THE PETERS SECOND BLACK AND BLUE GUIDE TO CURRENT LITERARY JOURNALS

With drawings
by
MEREDITH PETERS

Cherry Valley Editions
1985

Drawings throughout by Meredith Peters

Copyright c 1985 Robert Peters

Copyright c 1985 Meredith Peters

First edition.

ACKNOWLEDGEMENTS

Abbreviated versions of 3 of these essays
appeared earlier in THE SMALL PRESS REVIEW.

Library of Congress Cataloguing in Publication Data

Peters, Robert, 1924-
   The second Peters black &blue guide to current
         literary journals.
      Includes index.
      1. American poetry--20th century--History and
criticism--Addresses, essays, lectures. 2. American
poetry--Periodicals--Handbooks, manuals, etc.
I. Peters black and blue guide to current literary
journals. II, Title.   III. Title: Second Peters
black and blue guide to current literary journals.
PS615.P396 1985   811'.54'09   84-19998
ISBN 0-916156-76-1 (pbk.)

Beach & Company, Publishers
(Cherry Valley Editions)
3510 Olympic St
Silver Spring, MD 20906

<u>JOURNALS EXAMINED</u>

JOURNALS EXAMINED: THE FIRST BLACK AND BLUE GUIDE

<u>ABRAXAS</u>
<u>APR</u>
<u>ANTAEUS</u>
<u>BOXCAR</u>
<u>CHELSEA</u>
<u>CHICAGO REVIEW</u>
<u>FIELD</u>
<u>GEORGIA REVIEW</u>
<u>HUDSON REVIEW</u>
<u>IOWA REVIEW</u>
<u>KAYAK</u>
<u>KENYON REVIEW</u>
<u>REVIEW</u>
<u>THE NEW YORKER</u>
<u>OHIO REVIEW</u>
<u>POETRY</u>
<u>POETRY NORTHWEST</u>
<u>POETRY NOW</u>
<u>PUSCHART PRIZES:VII</u>
<u>QUARTERLY REVIEW OF</u> LITERATURE
<u>SALMAGUNDI</u>
<u>SHENANDOAH</u>
<u>SOUTHERN POETRY REVIEW</u>
<u>SOUTHERN REVIEW</u>

<u>TELEPHONE</u>
<u>VIRGINIA QUARTERLY</u>
<u>WORMWOOD REVIEW</u>

Poetry

FOURTEEN POEMS
SONGS FOR A SON
THE SOW'S HEAD AND OTHER POEMS
EIGHTEEN POEMS
BYRON EXHUMED
RED MIDNIGHT MOON
CONNECTIONS: IN THE ENGLISH LAKE DISTRICT
HOLY COW: PARABLE POEMS
COOL ZEBRAS OF LIGHT
BRONCHIAL TANGLE, HEART SYSTEM
THE GIFT TO BE SIMPLE: A GARLAND FOR ANN LEE
        FOUNDER OF THE SHAKERS
THE POET AS ICE-SKATER
GAUGUIN'S CHAIR: SELECTED POEMS
HAWTHORNE
THE DROWNED MAN TO THE FISH
CELEBRITIES: IN MEMORY OF MARGARET DUMONT
THE PICNIC IN THE SNOW: LUDWIG II OF BAVARIA
MAD LUDWIG OF BAVARIA: A PLAY
WHAT DILLINGER MEANT TO ME
HAWKER
KANE

Criticism and Editions

THE CROWNS OF APOLLO: SWINBURNE'S PRINCIPLES OF
        LITERATURE AND ART
PIONEERS OF MODERN POETRY (with George Hitchcock)
VICTORIANS ON LITERATURE AND ART
THE GREAT AMERICAN POETRY BAKE-OFF: FIRST and
        SECOND SERIES
THE PETERS BLACK AND BLUE GUIDE TO CURRENT
        LITERARY PERIODICALS
THE LETTERS OF JOHN ADDINGTON SYMONDS
GABRIEL: A POEM BY J. A. SYMONDS
J. A. SYMONDS: A PROBLEM IN GREEK ETHICS, etc.
EDMUND GOSSE: A JOURNAL
VICTORIANS ON LITERATURE AND ART
THE LOST GHABALS
THE COLLECTED POEMS OF AMNESIA GLASSCOCK (J. Steinbeck)
TAKAHASHI: THE COLLECTED POEMS
INTRODUCTIONS FOR Jonathan Williams, Jerry Ratch,
Carolyn Stoloff, David Ray, Edwin Honig, Rochelle
Ratner, Charles Plymell, Robin Magowan, Simon Perchick,
and Kathleen Spivak in the Scarecrow Press POETS NOW
Series.

"It is the critic's BUSINESS . . .to lure the reader.
Caviar, vodka, any hodge-podge of oddities that arouses
hunger or thirst is pardonable to the critic."

--Ezra Pound, "Examples of Civilization"

<u>FROM</u> <u>THEIR</u> <u>MOUTHS</u> <u>YE</u> <u>SHALL</u> <u>KNOW</u> <u>THEM</u>

"He'd rather have me as I was before."--<u>Sally</u> <u>Croft</u>, THE
BELLINGHAM REVIEW.

"Worse luck."--<u>Madeline</u> <u>De</u> <u>Frees</u>, GRAHAM HOUSE REVIEW.

"And the boy belongs to her / who drives his toast..."--
<u>Craig</u> <u>Raine</u>, GRAND STREET.

"What kind of fundamental tail has a pig really got?"--
<u>John</u> <u>Taylor</u>, GYPSY.

"This water is full of dogs."--<u>Laura</u> <u>Mullen</u>, IRONWOOD.

"I prayed to be / as unremembered as the dirt."--<u>Susan</u>
<u>Mitchell</u>, IRONWOOD.

"I want you to know I am loyal."--<u>Lucile</u> <u>Adler</u>, THE
MASSACHUSETTS REVIEW.

"Shirley clucks a little...."--<u>William</u> <u>Dickey</u>, NEW
LETTERS.

"Notice that oil pooling around the pond."--<u>Jack</u> <u>Heflin</u>,
PERMAFROST.

"The monotone of the dull rains of December."
--<u>Constance</u> <u>Urdang</u>, THE POETRY REVIEW

"Times Square is a blowjob."--<u>Hugh</u> <u>Fox</u>, PULPSMITH

"I have forgotten what I wanted to say."--<u>Michael</u>
<u>Garcia-Simms</u>, TELESCOPE.

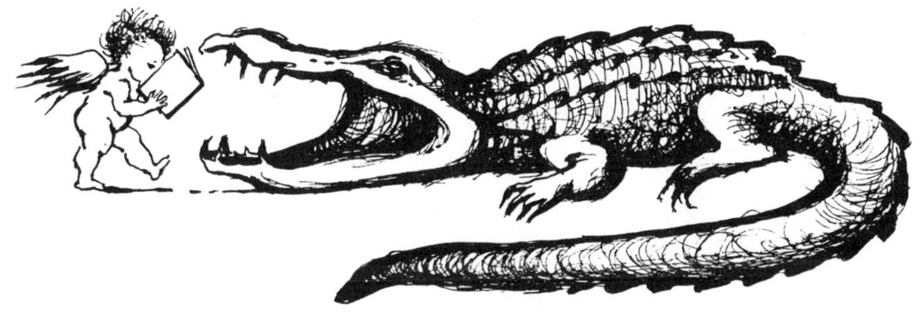

INTRODUCTION

The enthusiasm greeting the first PETERS BLACK AND
BLUE GUIDE TO CURRENT LITERARY JOURNALS (1983)
encourages us to proceed with a second GUIDE. Here
twenty-two new periodicals are examined.

My design remains the same: to scrutinize the
poetry in a selection of journals both fledgling and
hoary, both rambunctious and conservative. Again, in
the interests of space, I exclude fiction, essays, and
most of the reviews. This decision remains difficult,
for we certainly need acute assessments of the prose. I
do depart here from one earlier policy--not to include
magazines that have published my poetry and prose. My
poems have appeared in over a hundred journals, and my
essays would increase that number greatly. It seems
unfair to penalize those editors who have liked my work
enough to publish it. I realize, of course, that my
subconscious self tips towards those journals; yet, I
hope that by being clear about this, and by trying to be
objective, I am a responsible critic. Both IRONWOOD and
GYPSY, magazines I birch, have published me. On the
other hand, BLUEFISH, SULFUR, CONTACT II, SAMISDAT, and
NEW LETTERS get good scores.

My audience is three-fold: 1). librarians who seek
guidance through a maze of literary magazines. 2). Poets
looking for outlets who by reading the GUIDE may save
postage by sending work to mags that might possibly
publish them. THE PARIS REVIEW and THE MASSACHUSETTS
REVIEW read like conservative closed shops--and rarely
publish poets without substantial reputations. On the
other hand, if you don't write feisty poems that exploit
boundaries of form and theme forget SAMISDAT, CONTACT
II, and BOGG. 3). The host of poets who appear in the
GUIDE, either written large or small. Over 400 poets
are in the Index, an increase over the first GUIDE.

My taste is eclectic. I am just as excited by a
poem in an old form as I am by one that seems new.
Alfred Corn, for example, writes marvellously in the
manner of the Victorian poet George Meredith (THE PARIS
REVIEW). In the very different Projective Verse mode is
Paul Christensen's "The Nap," appearing in SULFUR. John
Engman (TELESCOPE) is a real master of the Wright-
Stafford Plain Folks Poem. I like these three poets
immensely.
     I continue to do battle with most that the ANTAEUS-
IOWA-APR-AWP-WESLEYAN AXIS represents: the Ego Poem

memorializing trivialities in a poet's life; the Old Folks At Home poem--excursions into sentimental memories of family and friends, and a poet's cute rites-of-passage; the Reportage Style, in which poems generate themselves around tedious journal entries; and the Academic Abroad Poem. My efforts to whack the bottoms of poets who write these poems badly (there are some who have mastered them) will seem obvious to even the casual reader.   If I offend the latter, I shall be pleased; for I hope to upset, amuse, and titillate--sufficiently to send readers off in quest of the journals and the poets I discuss. Certainly, I hope to encourage poets, particularly young ones who are not yet ossified into Workshop Clones. My final wish is that all readers, including those vehemently disagreeing with me, will appreciate the fact that I have tried to substantiate my judgments by evidence from poems themselves.

Once again, I employ Meredith Peters' drawings to embellish the book. If we were really up-to-date, the cover design of harpies typing at their Selectric with their toes (harpies don't have hands) should feature a Word Processor. The AWARDS colophon of the shaggy child holding a dead rabbit by its ears is reversed from what it was in the first GUIDE: here, the better the magazine the fewer noisome bunnies it receives.

Robert Peters
Huntington Beach, California
August 1984

<u>THE BELLINGHAM REVIEW</u>

Vol. 7:No.1 (Spring 1984).   Editor: Knute Skinner.
Associate Editor: Stan Hodson. 412 N. State,
Bellingham, WA 98225. $4 per year. $10.50 for three
years.

THE BELLINGHAM REVIEW exists primarily for poetry.
While this issue contains 2 short stories and a pair of
brief reviews, over half of the pages are devoted to
poems. Despite some deficiencies, the editors succeed
in putting together some most readable work. There's a
democratic flow throughout--prestigious names count for
little--the quality of the work determines appearances.
As a result, most of the poets are relatively unknown,
many publish only in the smallest of the small presses,
and are from all corners of the country.

The poems favored by Skinner are primarily of
direct personal experiences, of the sort made famous (or
infamous, depending on your point of view) by the
network of writing programs around the country. These
poems are ego-centered; I's float unabashedly through
the lines like winking fire-flies. Personal histories
of childhood and adolescence are favored--remembering
dad, grandma, a first date, and how awkward I was when
mom dropped her towel on leaving her bath. A couple of
the poets say it well: <u>Joyce Savre</u> in a memory of her
"hairy sister" Charlie sees a poem as "a slice of
reality, a log in the eye." Robert E. Lawson
characterizes his work as a "self-journal." His "Blind
Date," written in prose set out in lines resembling
poems, luxuriates in his dumbness on a date with a girl.
He sits with her in his car: "immobile, impotent with
uncertainty."

Other puppy-love poems are by <u>Maurice Scully</u>
("Margaret Dunne. / I name you for the magic of it, /
Your marvellous school uniform / Still on.") and <u>John
Davis</u>: Oh, how he loved his Fourth-Grade teacher <u>Miss
Gardner</u>.

Even poems departing from the Experiential Mode
quickly turn plebian. <u>Sally Croft</u>'s imaginative "Eve:
Reminiscence" transforms the Ur-Mother (she's been
expelled with Adam from Paradise) into a chatty, urbane,
laid-back lady. Here's the ending:

    Look at my hands,
    palms rough as his.
    He'd rather have me as I was before,

all soft, smelling of wild ginger.
I like him better now.
I wish I could tell him.
I wish he'd look at me and see me.
He never does. He looks over my head.
If I told him I loved him,
he wouldn't hear me. I wish he'd live
here and forget that other place.

Nicholas Rinaldi, meditating over a painting by Henri Rousseau, also works within the mode. While his diction and tone are not as casual as Croft's, and his lines are more compact and better rifted with imagery, he is never abstruse. A reader knows where he is at all times, even during the metaphysical close.

A few poems are erotic, but blandly so. None of the administrators of Washington State Bellingham could possibly be offended, unless Fabian Worsheim's account of making love in her "little-girl bed" with all its lavender and lace pillow shams and ruffles might upset them; or Val Gerstle's "An Army of Pleased Penises"; or, New York City poet Hal Sirowitz's excursions into of his parents' sexuality: his father as an aficionado of porn movies; his mother summoning him in to retrieve her bar of soap. She drops her towel, on purpose, to excite him. That night Sirowitz takes his own bath, but keeps his underwear on. The soaked clothes clinging to his body feel "like a second skin."

Pauline Palmer also parades personal intimacies: she's in bed. It's 4 a.m. and her cat sits on her chest licking her chin. She goes "to pee," petting the cat, who seems to be in her lap now. Puss doesn't distinguish between Palmer's grumbles and his purrs. This is amusing, but ephemeral. Another Ego-poet is Al Masarik His friends are puzzled because he doesn't seem to be himself. Well, his "heart has died" and "its ashes are blowing everywhere." He'll accept his egocentricity--for that's where the poems come from: "the poem is living proof / an avocado sprouting / from a shot glass."

One of the freshest of these proletariat poems is "How the Lovers Met," by Anthony Sobin. The poet falls in love with a female butcher at the local Safeway. The conversion of the cliché "breaking ice" is lovely. Here is the poem:

In the Safeway three days running now
he touches eyes with the blonde girl

in the white, bloodstained apron. How shy
they both are, how reluctant to smile.

But see, for an instant, how time stops;
to please him, she runs a shelf of ribs

through the band saw--
the sound of ice breaking.

The unpretentiousness of THE BELLINGHAM REVIEW is winning. While it is no ground-breaker, it performs well. If only some of our more self-important, glossier journals would take a few cues.

BLUEFISH

Vol 1: No. 1 (Autumn 1983). Editor: Anselm Parlatore. POB 1601, Southampton, L.I., NY 11968. $6 for 2 issues.

After an interlude of six years, GRANITE reappears complete with new format and name. The journal ran for a dozen issues (1971-1977), while the editors George M. Young, Gail Besemer, and Anselm Parlatore were at Dartmouth College. Each issue of GRANITE was fat, focusing exclusively on poetry, interviews, and reviews. Many of the poets were either students or teachers at Cornell, where Parlatore was an undergraduate: Ammons, Matthews, Morgan and Bertolino were all Cornellites. Seven books were published (and are still available from BLUEFISH): Anthologies of New Hampsire and Vermont poets; TEN JAPANESE POETS (translated by Hiroaki Sato and featuring Takahashi whose work was later published by Evergreen Review Press and more recently by Crossing

Press); and early books by Theodore Enslin, James Bertolino, Russell Banks, and Robert Peters. Towards the end of its run, GRANITE received some unsought publicity. The cro-magnon governor of New Hampshire, Meldrim Thompson, glanced through GRANITE and found a poem about castrating a cat. He was greatly offended and forced the State Arts Council to withdraw a grant they had awarded to Parlatore. The case became a cause célebre, as it deserved to, in the poetry world.

Eventually, Parlatore, who served as the primary editor for GRANITE, moved to Long Island, built a house, established his practice, kept writing his own poems, and has now launched BLUEFISH. This first BLUEFISH reunites many GRANITE poets. Most of them are writing better than ever; and some have achieved reknown: James Bertolino, Siv Cedering, Edward Butscher, William Matthews, Robert Morgan, Simon Perchik, Allen Planz, and Charles Simic. A few of the old standards appear, and are still writing well: William Stafford, David Ignatow, and A. R. Ammons.

Stafford and Ammons lead off. Stafford is among the most obliging of poets who send work to help fledgling journals. I am hoping to see an editor, though, with the courage to put Stafford somewhere else than on pageone. Stafford's "Sentences", appearing here, is one of his best poems. He recalls being in prison. a "closing in" of horrendous proportions (understated by Stafford). Much that is adverse spells its name for us: "Whatever is closing toward us begins to spell/its name, clouds, it says, or wind." Some of what transpires we welcome; much we do not:

In prison, where I once was, all the hours that came
brought a partner that was their own--it was
    almost like
a sound, but then it didn't quite lift or arrive.

The term was for 4 years, and all he heard was age and lonely time.

A. R. Ammons, alas, is weak. He meanders as he so often does, and, to use his concluding observation about the world, his poem "is a sort of place, highly / designated, and empty."

Robert Morgan, master of the Home Poem/Nature Poem in the Stafford/Frost manner, contributes four poems and a definitive critical piece on Russell Edson, along with some first rate speculations on the nature of the prose poem. Over the years, Morgan has quietly and persistently fashioned remarkable poems. His craftsmanship is always secure, and he is never sentimental or phoney. When it comes to your basic grandmother, mother, father, dead uncle, lost brother poem (all woeful genres in contemporary verse) Morgan writes rings around nearly every one else. His "Uncle Robert" displays many of his virtues. His Uncle died in England during WW II when his B-17 crashed. Morgan inherited souvenirs, and was told by his family that he was "marked" by his uncle. Not only was he given the uncle's name, but young Robert seemed to his relatives "actually" to be the uncle. He shared a stammer, had the uncle's paintings on his bedroom wall, kept one of his poems in a box with old ration books, and shared a spot in the woods where the Uncle loved to read, paint, and sleep. His old canoe, stored in the barnloft, frightened young Robert: each time he turned it he feared he'd find a body:

> It lay among the shucks
> and fodder as though washed up by a flood
> and stranded forever.

This passage displays Morgan's strengths: the intimate tone, the descriptive eye, the imagery fraught with intense emotion, the transcendental overtones. Morgan is on a testimonial quest after his own identity, via his uncle's. That he fails to produce resonance from an old bugle is at best an approximate success:

> One day I found your bugle
> in the attic, velveted with dust and lint.
> The brass felt damp with corrosion,
> the bell dented and dark as leather.
> I took it out behind the house and,
> facing west, blew into the cold mouthpiece
> a hopeful syllable. The metal trembled
> and blared like a sick steer, went quiet.
> I poured all the body heat into the barrel
> and a sour flatulence shook out and echoed
> off the mountains. I made half-musical
> squeaks and bursts till dizzy, aiming vowels
> like watermelon seeds into the tub.
> When the groans returned from Buzzard Rock
> I thought they must be wails from the cove
> for someone dead, and nothing I had sent,
> or the ghost of a train lost in the valley
> or relayed like an aural mirage from
> the past still with us and talking back.

William Matthews writes a rather bad-tempered poem about how lucky he is to be rid of a past entanglement, perhaps a marriage. As usual, there's an impressive technical sheen. Charles Simic imagines the problems you'd have trying to crucify yourself. Simic's plebian touches are there--the worn shoe, the chair with the loose leg. His sick-joke victim succeeds in nailing one hand to the wall, then decides he wants a last smoke (he is in no obvious pain), so he reaches for a butt. The final lines are a shoddy attempt at symbolism and "fine" writing. He helps himself to the butt

> Which he can't quite manage to light,
> And the night coming, the deft night.

The last line is a dismal cop-out.

The _Ignatow_ family, _David, Rose_, and _Yaedi_ appear. Yaedi needs to work on her grammar and lean out her lines. "I wished we were them....I wished we were calm like them." _Jane Somerville_ writes a fine essay on James _Bertolino_. Bertolino is a striking, elusive, and disturbing poet. He must be pleased with Somerville's essay; it's a helpful way into Bertolino's five poems. His view of the world is both saturnine and ugly. Foetus, slugs, malformed humans, birth-monsters, and genetically damaged animals, all produce a Boschian commentary on a 1980's gone beserk. One reads Bertolino feeling that Armageddon is well underway. He arraigns the human organism (in "Posterity Will Never Know") for sanctioning its destructive instincts via mysticism/prophecy:

> We sought the wobbling cipher
> which devolved itself a brain,
> but found instead the weapon of prophecy.
> Suddenly our motives were blandly acceptable,
> like television, or killing Jews.
>
> We built then the original "system of error"
> into the biosphere. We gained all but
> a community large enough
> to dissipate our guilt.
>
> We are the genetic malingerers,
> aline organelles in the Body Mystical.

Once we have destroyed ourselves, "oily beetles" and centipides will keep marching, dancing, "bearing their ancient genes / to the new age of insect destiny." No poet I know has such a view, and writes of it so compellingly. By contrast, _Simic_'s recent poems are antimicassar work.

Parlatore himself writes a poem rifted with pre-historic viscosities, silicate melts, magma punctures, animal bone fossils, "stranded beach dune systems." His world, like Bertolino's, is on a swift return to primal sludge and vertebral remains.   Parlatore is unique in his incorporation of language from medicine into poems. This delights me. Most Americans who read are lazy, and they'll dismiss you if you use words they don't know.

Melina Costello, a student of Bertolino's, writes in his shadow. "Angelus" is dedicated to him, and reflects a mix of Bertolinonean body flaw / blister, first gulpings for air, and flowers and church towers. Costello tries too hard. Here she inverts the mother's milk idea, sending the milk (and perhaps the baby) back into mom's nipple:

> This is eucharist & red long after
> the arms have swum back thru her milk
> joyous for a supple death.

Marie Harris writes of deficiencies in her Catholic girlhood, in "Tableaux." She tried hard to be obedient, and when she had her first child, she was not well-prepared: "I am very young / and without skills." Edward Butscher turns a surrealist image of "moon poem" into "a shiver of undone tinfoil / to slit your sardine throat." The shimmer works. To paraphrase him: There's "no fooling around." In "Greek Lesson," he slits a cloud, removes its cobalt lining, gently cracks "each whale rib / with Nazi-thick thumbs" and extracts its complex heart. Then, on to childhood recollections, and a son, "a blond oracle" alone in a field plotting "tiger fires" and "resurrection." Butscher is a brilliant biographer (he's finishing up one on Conrad Aiken), and has a brainy and exciting essay here on Robert Nozik's PHILOSOPHICAL EXPLANATIONS.

James Grabill writes self-consciously, and at some length, about the poetry he finds in jays, throbbing pods, dock labor: "the poem / rising out of the earth and standing up into someone." Graham Everett contributes a couple of passable night/winter nature poems. They are lean and almost compelling: winter fog gets so thick, the air "throws your own light / back." Ron Overton wields a skillful minimalist style to put the enormous threats of the universe in perspective: have sex under a lightbulb with three positions, buy soap, re-stamp your library books. These things are "not much," he admits. But he does keep going:

> There is the pleasure of a clean shirt,
> the need at dusk for light.

John Latta seems to track the Language Poets; or, perhaps he is one of the cats they are busy tracking. Here's a representative passage: "I take the amaranth for its constancy, the day // lily for its fatuous fealty of muster, o yes, / I do too....

And earlier: "I smushed / a cockroach. The littlest whelp of feeling." Perhaps I'm wrong--Latta's following what sounds more like a Joycean rather than a Language Poet spoor.

R. B. Weber writes an opening line in its badness equal to any by that other notorious writer of initial bad lines, Matthew Arnold. Here's Weber's: "My eyes squeeze water into hot sand." Simon Perchik is a fine poet obsessed with the colon (the mark of punctuation), and contributes elusively-expressed recollections of childhood with style. Siv Cedering steps refreshingly outside the first-person poem, in a six-part "Guillermo's Wedding," fraught with blood and passion, reminiscent of Lorca.

Finally, Allen Planz's "Woodknot" commemorates "scartissue" as an image how life sears us. Scartissue is hard to break:

                    Ligaments
                  & tendons
            snap with bone, twist thru muscle
        but this torque gnarled with wire & horn
            gives way only to fire,
                  & that last.

The liver casing of a shark he throws into a meatgrinder is also tough: "it writhed/unscathed in coils of steel." As he retrieves the skin from the boatdeck, he notes a scar knotting his arm--which leads on to the "woodknot," from which "a shadow never strays." The whorl of the knot points downcountry, toward home. Planz relates all this with the toughness of a Thoreau:

        Even the hardest texts
            fracture
        in the stress of their own making.

The closing stanzas are a beautiful interweaving of human scars, endurance, and Planz's own future:

        Thumbjoint
    cantilevered into arthritic archways,
        winch clutch suddenly unfreezing,
                chainsaw
        shying away from a cedar hip in deadly
            abrupt recoil:

        these things I can take
            only in rest
          that rust
        in which I hear myself snoring,

        by which I keep tuned
    all the scars crossing my voicebox
        but one
    torchcut by my captain spinning the wheel.

    This is an impressive BLUEFISH.   Obviously,
Parlatore has access to a vast number of fine writers;
so he doesn't need much window-dressing from Stafford,
Ignatow, and Ammons.

BOGG 52

(1984). Editors: John Elsberg (422 N. Cleveland St.,
Arlington, VA 22201); George Cairncross (31 Belle Vue
St., Filey, N. Yorkshire YO14 9HU, England); Robert
Boyce, 48 Academy Ave., Mulgrave, Victoria 3170,
Australia). $3 per copy; $7.50 for 3 issues.

    BOGG is rare for a number of reasons: it features both
American poetry, short fiction, and reviews and similar
work from England, Canada, and Australia.   It is
inexpensively produced. It has a lengthy history (this
is issue 52). It is lively and prints poets both known
and unknown--prestige and big reputations don't impress
these editors much--and that's refreshing. And it has
special sections devoted to letters from readers and
contributors, both negative and positive.

The British chunk, though generally better-written than the American, seems pallid by comparison. Britisher Mike Johnson complains that the U. S. work "is still amazingly obsessed with sexual variations." A Canadian, Sheila Martindale, admires BOGG's "great balance between intelligent and slightly loony--super reading." Dave Steward finds "pretty drifty stuff" in the British half. And so it goes.

BOGG's drift is hairy. One detects old Bukowski's boozy droll breath on many of the pages. An "old joke" provides Tom Bilicke with a Senryu: moth balls help make baby moths. Lyn Lifshin boasts of her sheer pink nipples, and seeks to perpetrate her self-generating myth that she's a sex-machine by penalizing her men for "early withdrawal." Editor Elsberg's wet dream produces a "protean woman." A tits and ass bit from Gerald Dorset: "Her broad thighs encase / the sliding oval of her belly / as our conversation drifts / from Plato to her bare midriff." Todd Moore teaches his girl to shoot beer cans off fence posts. Standing behind her, swooning over her perfume and snatch smell, Moore has a hard-on that won't quit. Miriam Cohen wants to have eyes "radiating / cinematic lines / stunningly vulgar." Ron Androla, anxious to jack off while leering at the woman across the way who blocks him out via sheets at the window, manages a good look from upstairs, and proceeds. Androla, one of the nastiest of these poets, supplies this little gem:

JOHNNY CASH

i love munching on a
chilled bull-frog between
2 slices of burnt toast

James Sallis writes of Albert who once screwed a woman who "glowed in the dark": "It was like sticking your dick in a light socket,/ screwing the northern lights."

Several excellent poems have little or nothing to do with droll sex, demand more than an easy, single-read, and for quality match up with any appearing in current literary magazines. In "Riches," Steve Richmond, a much under-rated poet who has been around since the 50's, reads his Poe, and manages to accommodate having been ripped off by artists who plead distress, borrow money, and never pay it back. Degeneration of creative talents (Poe was a model) is Richmond's theme: one of his painters sits in the gutter "waiting for a businessman / to drive by with fifty bucks / for a couple of bags." A conga drummer is totally burned out on junk, valium, methadone, and booze. Simon Perchik contributes a poem on his father, occasioned by his holding a penny he'd received from his dad. As Perchik ages, so does the memory:

>   My floor stained :no blood
>   is this endless, no air
>   more lush, darkening forever
>   his penny, his touch.

Michael Allen and Maura Liebman write touching and straightforward poems on failed love. Liebman thinks she has patched things up with her dude, has a good time with him at a lake, but then he slams the door in her face. Allen writes of his fears that he won't have it right when a lover appears. Here is the entire poem:

>   I am always beginning. Yesterday it was this,
>   today it's three wild violets and a green dish
>   of water.
>   I cannot get them right for your arrival, somehow--
>   they keep floating off--nothing will stay arranged.
>   I have revised myself so many times I am thin
>   as a blade.
>   Peeling the fat, excessive potatoes,
>   I throw out protective skins and coatings--
>   keep what I can eat only, snipping unedible stems
>   from green beans.
>   My favorite thing's a paring knife, now.
>   And I have given all the clothes away that
>   weren't loose enough,
>   keeping a yellow shirt and half-white jeans.
>
>   I never will be naked enough for you.

Barbara Lefcowitz' lengthy "My Poetry Retirement Dinner" has several moments of bright humor; the piece is a natural poetry-reading crowd-pleaser. Some spots don't quite work: viz., sonnets "doing yoga / to stretch their spines"; calling one's poems long-distance on their birthdays. Harold Witt's George Morton, the manager of a tacky Citrus Empire Hotel, in Visalia, California, reports on his dismal life, and concludes: "Most of the time this place is so dull / you can hear the flies pass gas."

A Ron Androla page (Androla edits the outrageous and randy NORTHERN PLEASURE) features 5 poems from a collection THE KISS published by BOGG, as one of the latter's free-for-postage chapbook series. In this one, "Seagulls," Androla flirts with murder:

>   i'd eventually
>
>   hover like a

> small feathered devil
>
> over yr sun-tanned
> belly, tender as
>
> wet fish,
> regurgitated bread,
>
> my beak
> ripping for sweet blood.

Androla's "Against My Word" is filled with Rabelasian surprises: shit perfume, a skinned rat, claustrophobia, head-ache exhaustion, and valium depression. Here is the poem:

> old lemon light, late summer exhaustion
> stuck in a hole of a room. all my
> headaches & raw pork stomach smelling
> shit perfume under the sun with warm
> whiff up the sides of a slow face like
> valium ugliness, excessive green
> fresh-cut grass groans below in the
> yards like a skinned rat in a capped
> bottle on the window-sill. static fur
> fingers crackle on a blue machine,
>
> yellow clouds shift slow over oak trees
> as if creating what distance is.

Some of the British try too hard to write like the Americans. John Crix, for example, can't do much better than "show chicken-shit brake lights," as he goes careening through a mountain pass (he sees it as a sexy women). Sheila Martindale (interestingly, most of the women, English and American, seem to lack the inventive starch of the men) elaborates an off-game love thing as a tennis match: she boasts of her "reliable service" (good head-giver) and "ball control." Bernard Young as a tits and ass man is sophomoric:

> And here he is
> and he is thinking Legs!
> Legs! Legs! Legs!
> A leg man.
> Until he considers breasts.
> Breasts. Bosoms. Tits. Tit man.
> The undoing of the bra straps.
> Star-baps. Stab-raps. Brat-saps.

When Barrie Tilley throws in alliterations the result is god-awful: "The motorway panther / pumps her purling pistons," etc. Karen Buckland is woefully sentimental as

she waits for her boyfriend to phone...her hands are
shaking (cliché #1), she's keeping back the questions
she wants to ask (#2), and she is so loaded with hurt
she wants to cry (#3). Barry Edgar Pilcher's riff on a
poet as a "wordworm" who feeds his baby bits of
spaghetti is good. Australian poet Wilga Rose
contributes a lovely "Shoreline."

I won't comment much on the lively and numerous
reviews--BOGG is worth reading for these alone. Some
forty single-paragraph reviews, plus notices of over a
dozen magazines appear in the American section; and the
British half is equally rich.

Long may BOGG wave!

THE CONNECTICUT POETRY REVIEW

Vol. III: No. 1 (1984). Editors: Christine Sennett, J.
Clair White. Associate Editors: James Wm. Chichetto,
Dan Duffy, Agnes Pruzinsky, etc. Amity Station, New
Haven, CT 06525. $2 per copy.

This has to be one of the most lovingly produced
poetry magazines around: the issues are letter press and
Smythe sewn, and incorporate a variety of type sizes and
faces, reserving the largest and cleanest for the poems
themselves. The journal is a joy to read. And the
writing lives up to the format. The editors are open to
unknown poets; in fact, most of these poets are fairly
young, write in a variety of styles, and are
professional. There's rarely anything tired or
hackneyed.

CPR opens with a focus on Greg Kuzma's poetry, with
reviews by Dan Duffy and Mark Johnston, among others.
Three new poems by Kuzma bear out the qualities
discerned by the critics--lucidity; a stark love for

objects (usually rural) shared with <u>Charles Simic</u>; and his affectionate humanity. My favorite of Kuzma's poems is "Consciousness." Beside a river, he strips down to find a "tiny annoying stick" in his flesh. "Naked as a river," he stands, considering "the fallen chest, the shoulders / like some animal, hair turned / awkwardly, and belly aquiver/under the ribs." He seems to feel some uncanny relation with the primal ooze from which life "rose upward into consciousness."

A fine companion poem is <u>Clint McCown</u>'s "Bears." In this one, the bear gets away. Boys cut school, drive into the mountains, filling up on junk-food, mire their car, pick their way through the dark across three ridges, where they wait for dawn. The shelter they erect is worthy of hunters on safari. All day they wait, freeze, are left with

> imaginings
> of bears
> rampaging through the high school halls
> while we filled in for them here,
> the dangerous lives of the forest.

<u>Mark Johnston</u> swings too many generalities; viz., "the immortality of chance," names holding "promise," etc.; but there's something winning, perhaps because of his deft line-breaks and energy. In good <u>Robert Frostian</u> fashion, <u>Michael Finley</u> returns to his old family home, now in ruins, a place refreshingly "remote from the dangers" he met on the road driving there: a dead dog, an over-turned car. He falls asleep and is awakened by two hornets mating on his wrist, "a miracle." Alas, he winds off with a sentimentally, recalling <u>James Wright</u> at his worst:

> and I can't help thinking of my mother
> twenty years ago,
> shaking out rugs on the porch.

<u>Rochelle Ratner</u>'s "Finding the Words" eschews religious bigotry in dealing with parents over purchasing a rug. <u>James Sallis</u> mystifies me: his theme seems to be choosing whether or not to live one's life in Boston. You stay there, educate yourself; or, you take the river, or the trucks on their way to Cincinnati. Whatever you do, don't dream too much: "They used to hate / the way you carried the sky around / under your arm, you know."

<u>Lee Upton</u>'s "The Wives" is a fresh take on a rare domestic problem: a new wife lives in the apartment above her husband's former wife, and feels allied with the latter. At the start, she's unaware of the true

nature of the people downstairs, until a boy appears, says he is the husband's son, and asks that his train be fixed. Says the new wife: "I loved them both,/ your wife and son, wanted them near me more than I think / you did." The boy later brings a damaged mechanical lion, which can't be repaired. As the father tries, the two women stand nearby exchanging smiles. The mother and the boy convey to the new wife "a form of tenderness." There's a delicate twist at the end: the wife can't help siding with the first wife, "although," she tells her husband, "I have loved you." The husband must feel chilled. I like this poem.

On a boardwalk in San Diego, <u>Cynthia R. Golderman</u> meets a tall, rangy, beige man wearing tan cords, who walks as if his right leg were a fake. She wishes to avoid him, and gazes out at the sea. The man, though, holds out his hand--it's made of metal. So far, so good. Golderman fakes "a tan eternity" in the "soul of a tortured man." I don't believe it--she over-reaches, finding as <u>Matthew Arnold</u> did, that when your imagination flags throw in abstractions. This line is a nadir: "in the grasping / realizing of ineptitude, a falsity, / of hopelessness." Finally, her own bones are bleaching as she turns her eyes "to the blue-green sea's immensity." Poor <u>A. C. Swinburne</u>.

Two fresh, no-nonsense poems by <u>Felice Picano</u> follow. The first celebrates his birthmark, "a splatter of rash / two inches long" on his left bicep. He kisses it when he showers and touches it when he passes "obvious monsters." The thing burns at times, and when a lover sees it he remarks that it looks burnt..."burnt into life." The second, "Cain and Abel: An Update," transpires in an apartment where the speaker satisfies a "brother" by shooting him up with junk. A parable for the times.

<u>Francis Xavier Drapeau</u>'s "No Swimming" evokes some of the <u>Henry Vaughan</u>'s famous "Eternity." Taut projective verse lines contain vibrant imagery. At the outset, Drapeau compresses Earth and stars:

    I feel the slow   dry   grind
      of Earth on her axis. I miss you.
        that chalkboard squeal
          of hard-nail stars   sliding....

The sky, like "a lifeguard's silver glasses" stares down, sharing Drapeau's pain, "hooked through the upper lips / of two fish as they / flicker, like knives." Worse in power than the stars themselves is his anguish: the stars are incapable of freezing the "icy aluminum plane" of the pool; they can't fill that pool "the way you fill a / fist-size heart." He sees the lover jacknife, naked, off a slice of quarter-moon. He vanishes, slurping, swallowing and swimming "the whale-slate depth / between stars." Drapeau feels surcease-- and knows where the lover is. Drapeau is an impressive young writer.

Laurel Speer's "Rolling in From California" is too bizarre to believe. She opts for the easy effect: a dude drives into a yard where a woman waits. Beside him in the car sits his father shot dead, "his face bloodless / as a pig strung by its feet." The associations of butchered crittur seem sentimental and forced.

The much underrated Emilie Glen contributes a harrowing poem about a trip with a young son to visit the father dying in a VA hospital. The boy is generic American boy, complete with Star Wars book. It's winter--the Hudson is "in diamond chips." At the hospital, the husband makes Glen promise that he won't be stuck "in a military hole in the ground." She agrees to bury him near her mother in Rochester. The boy then asks to go to Niagara Falls; i.e., to get on with his life. Glen seems to be on his side, life-affirming:

> A deer rosy with sunset
>   at the edge of a field in snow,
> hawks overhead splitting the sky
>   with their outer wing feathers,
> Sing, we sing about knowing every inch of the way
>   from Albany to Buffalo.

W. D. Ehrhart's "Home is the Hunter," is a powerful poem about deer hunters flying back to Colorado from Indiana. The light plane comes in too low, almost crashes, clears some power lines:

> Then suddenly you nosed straight up
> 300 feet, stalling out, rolling right,
> the left wing flipping belly up
> before the final plunge,
> the tiny frail contraption
> crumpling
> on impact with the earth.

There are no survivors.

The weakest poems in this issue appear towards the end. Much published Walter McDonald is not impressive as he memorializes the struggle of aspen trees up a mountain. Better is his poem on owls and mice. Here is a good moment: "Field mice with round eyes / and rapidly beating hearts // look everywhere but up. / What lies above is moonlight / and has wings...." Laurel Trivelpiece stands "under stones" and meditates on tree frogs "typing out prayers." Judy Keyser wields the "you said" poem without any discernible distinction.

The journal closes with some incisive reviews of Paul Trachtenberg's SHORT CHANGES FOR LORETTA, a rare small book in the voice of an outrageous female who tries just about everything going; Christopher Bursk's LITTLE HARBOR, picked up from a volume published by QUARTERLY REVIEW OF LITERATURE; and an over-view of the Scarecrow Press POETS NOW SERIES, an on-going series that includes these poets: Jonathan Williams, Rochelle Ratner, Jerry Ratch, Edwin Honig, David Ray, and Carolyn Stoloff. The next poets in the series are Robin Magowan, Charles Plymell, Simon Perchick, and Kathleen Spivack.

CONTACT/II

Summer 1982. Editors: Maurice Kenny, J. G. Gosciak. POB
451, Bowling Green Station, New York, NY 10004.
Bimonthly. $8 per year.

CONTACT/II is one of the best of our available
outlets for alternative publishing. What makes this
journal outstanding is its professionalism--seen
primarily in the balance it creates between main-stream
American writers, ie., white writers, and Native
American, Chicano, Oriental, gay and lesbian, and
feminist writers. The 8 1/2 x 11 format, the generous
size of the print, and the superb graphics and
imaginative lay-out are other manifestations of its
professionalism. There are many reviews, primarily of
alternative and small press books. Here too there is
balance, between poetry, biography, and theory. The
poetry includes translations. Occasionally, most of an
entire issue is given over to a special group. The most
ambitious was a triple issue devoted to women's
writing--it sold out almost at once. The editors
obviously fulfilled a considerable need, at some risk to
the magazine itself. A triple issue means that the
journal appears only twice a year, instead of four
times; subscribers may feel short-changed. A
publication flourishes best if it appears regularly and
on time. This is an issue at the heart of alternative
and small-press journals--editors may save themselves
time and postage by doubling up numbers, issuing what in
fact are anthologies rather than regular issues of their
magazine. There are risks. I would urge journals to
stay on track, appear regularly, and establish a
reputation for reliability. Anthologies can then be
published as an offshoot enterprise--or what now appears
as a one-shot triple or double issue can be published
over two or three separate quarterly numbers.

CONTACT/II poets are a mix of the known and the
unknown. Gary Snyder contributes two poems written in
calligraphy; a good interview with Thom Gunn by Steve
Abbott is followed by a selection of new and selected
poems. The editors seem to prefer poems with a fairly
clear narrative design, with just the right mix of
elusive imagery to fix the reader's attention. There is
little evidence of any avant garde writing, and
celebrations of life are preferred to downers. Self-
pitying Ego Poets and Solipsists had better go
elsewhere.

In each issue there is controversy. Here regular poet/critic Arlene Stone defends herself against a spirited but not very enlightened attack by Susan L. Yung, who disagrees with Stone's assessment of an anthology of Asian women writers. Many helpful notices, in the nature of news briefs, feature new journals and books with a multi-cultural slant.

The quality of the poems is high. A sampling of first-lines foreshadows the energy present throughout. These are all by different poets:

"The baths burning / and no one admitting to smoke"

"The meadows give themselves up / to the sheriff"

"I broke into your house last night"

Salvatore Farinella writes a harrowing poem on being trapped on the seventh floor of a burning gay baths, which he relates to our being trapped in other life contexts. Kathy Epling creates a stalwart self-reliant woman enjoying her rural life with dog, child, and apples. Stimulated by the magic of falling winesaps the dog goes "crazy," the boy dances, "& / later we'll make pie." Paula Gunn Allen employs a refrain, "and sorrow is not to enter / into it," to control powerful emotions on losing a lover--or, so I read the narrative. She flirts with a journalistic style--plenty of first-person pronouns, easy abstractions; but she brings it off touchingly: "some things just // don't go on."

Joe Johnson employs an energetic argot for delineating some incredible sex:

    I break rooms and wrangle my thighs and vote
        for pain
    I turn and burn her mouth in my thighs...
    lonesome bones fooling sperms: black hard
        velvet rivers...

With this outrageous opening line, Johnson seems to be showing off more than he needs to: "I'm praying before the snatch of a sixteen year old girl." If you're into cunnilingus smeared with religion, this may be your dish. Johnson doesn't need to stack his deck so obviously. One of his most original passages is this one:

    freaks in souped down zion slipping glass in chiba
    bitch in heat with two time loser popping dougy
            "smack, joints and bags, hash red hash"
    shooting up blue horse

My favorite poem is <u>Larry</u> <u>Zirlin</u>'s panegyric to cookies. A marvellous dining room filled with pies, candies, fruit cakes, and cookies makes his teeth ache just to think of them. For good measure, he scatters "the thick scent of flowers" among the sweets. This stanza should drive any dessert-freak mad:

> The cookies, sprinkled heavily with powdered sugar
>   after they
> were arranged, do not really resemble a ski
>   slope. Removing
> the top cookie cause its ghost to appear atop
>   three cookies,
> whose ghosts are discerned on nine cookies,
>   & so forth.

A model for working an image throughout a poem is <u>Jemila</u>'s "The Mirrors." Her life is fraught with mortal difficulties:

> the mirrors tilted and began to shine
> maliciously, as if about to give away my secrets
> but made no announcements in his presence, only
> shivered cruelly in my dreams that night

Eventually, as the seasons progress and winter arrives, the mirror shatters.

Among lesser efforts is <u>Herman</u> <u>Gold</u>'s "Everybody is Buried in A Pauper's Grave." The lines meander much as the "midnight cat" meanders into the pauper's coffin. The language is pretentious, whether or not we believe that Gold is indeed in his coffin talking to us. He's "happy to be moving," he informs us, "where sadness is unknown / and the only ordinance" is that statues of artists "be erected in every square." He almost brings it off though, when he envisions the "new sky" with its "fresh earth," "smell of quiet" and "worms swimming gracefully." <u>Harley</u> <u>Joens</u> is busily trying to pull up trees, after they have been <u>greened</u> by spring. I guess he's so frustrated by a running <u>hippie</u> girl he takes it out on nature: "in spring / in my mind / Susan still runs barefoot / through those Osceola hills." Finally, I must admit I can't get excited over <u>Marianne</u> <u>Andrea</u>'s "Detachments" (she asks for <u>T. S. Eliot</u>'s blessing). These abstractions,"enmeshed in vasteness (sic), "watched silence," "stately posture," are very hollow boys.

<u>Thom</u> <u>Gunn</u>'s poems are good. He is clear, lean, and always the empathetic observer. In "Outside the Diner," bums feed off garbage papers, sleep in abandoned cars, visit the Detox Clinic. "Iron Landscapes" commemorates Gunn's fascination with the girders of bridge and ferry

in New York City, an "iron landscape," with the Statue of Liberty, that "tiny woman in the mist" in the harbor. In "Dolly," a pathetic man who was deprived of dolls as a child grows up to play with all of them he wants, only they are crippled, quadriplegics:

> I know someone who
> was never let play with dolls
> when he was little, so now
> (he thinks to spite his father)
> collects them.
> But it's the crippled ones
> he cherishes most, particularly
> the quadriplegics: they loll
> blank stomachs depending from blank heads
> with no freedom
>   ever, ever
> and in need.

"Courage, A Tale" recounts the fears of a boy who understands that on his one hundredth masturbation he'll die. "Fuck it," he decides, "it's worth dying for," and in half an hour the count rises from 99 to 105.

Gary Snyder's poems have since appeared in AXE-HANDLES. The better one is "Old Woman Nature," a marvellously playful mix of woodsy details, a scary old witch woman, and some soup she is making, possibly from mouse heads, fox scat, bone flakes, and cartilage bits, retrieved by her from the woods.

The reviews in this issue are largely positive: Andrew Wiget on Simon Ortiz; Neil Baldwin on Paul Mariani's biography of William Carlos Williams; Rochelle Ratner on Kathleen Norris. Less positive is Geary Hobson on Keith Wilson's THE SHAMAN DEER; Maurice Kenny on Dick Higgins' OF CELEBRATIONS OF MORNING; Neil Baldwin on Philip Dacey; Steve Abbott on Robert Hershon; and Joseph Keppler on William Pillin's Selected Poems. And there are several more reviews. Baldwin praises Mariani's massive biography of Williams, but with these reservations: fine interpretative passages throughout the book are "frustrating tidbits." Whenever "Mariani fortuitiously hits upon the right relationship between subject and analysis, the result gives a tantalizing hint of what this book could well have been." Williams remains elusive: "the absolute materials of his life," Baldwin concludes, "remain unmastered."

Later issues of CONTACT/II are on a par with this one. I'll believe that literature is in good shape when CONTACT/II turns up on all the newstands in the country.

m. peters

<u>ELECTRUM</u>

No. 33 (Summer 1984). Editors: Bart Yoder. Roger Suva.
Associate Editors: John Brander. Julia Stein. 1435
Louise St., Santa Ana, CA 92706.

ELECTRUM is a local magazine, one that's been
around for years, that has recently gone professional.
What makes its presence so important is that it
flourishes in Orange County, California, a region of the
U. S. hitherto famed for cultural moribundity. All this
is changing. Within the past half-dozen years the
County has come alive: it will soon boast one of the
major legitimate theater complexes in the U. S., will
have a major art museum, and a first-rate music
facility. ELECTRUM is part of this movement. For the
first time, Orange County poets have a real literary
journal.

The bulk of this issue, as one would expect, is
devoted to Southern Californians. And there is a
fascinating mix--few journals are as catholic in their
taste. There are Asians, whites, blacks, Chicanos
(published bi-lingually), university poets, street
poets, <u>Charles Bukowski</u> and followers, ecology and anti-
nuclear poems, political poems, old poets, young poets
(one of the best of these is 18 year old <u>Wendy
Rasmussen</u>). Among notable writers outside the area is
<u>Billy Collins,</u> of New York, who contributes "The Dead
Ringer," a poem in the pop, cool, funky manner:

        He is the only man to have won
        25 different look-alike contests
        in one year without even entering.

        In public, everyone confuses him
        with everyone else.
        Aren't you Ghandi? Ringo? Philip Roth?
        the autograph seekers ask

        realizing as he signs their books
        that he even resembles them.

        He suffers more mistaken identities
        daily than Shakespeare arranged
        in a lifetime

        and he is sick of his lack of self,
        the nights spent trying to razor
        his face off the mirror
        like an expired parking sticker,

34

never once being hailed as Tom,
which is his name.

He is consoled only by the beautiful
wives and girlfriends of other men,
the ones who stop him on the street
with smiles honeying their faces and say,
"I thought you were at work, sweetheart."

Utterly different is a lengthy surrealist poem by Ivan
Arguelles, of Berkeley. Nellie Wong contributes a
harrowing and spare account of what growing up in
Oakland was like:

                    ...I felt ashamed
of some yellow men, their small bones,
their frail bodies, their spitting
on the streets, their coughing,
their lying in sunless rooms,
shooting themselves in the arms....

when I was growing up, I felt
dirty. I thought that god
made white people clean
and no matter how much I bathed,
I could not change, I could not shed
my skin in the gray water....

While there are a number of weak poems, generally from
local poets, forthcoming issues should be stronger as
word spreads and poets outside the area send good work
here. A word on the format: it's very uncluttered,
tasteful, with numerous graphics, features small photos
of most of the poets, and has a modest review section
which reproduces the covers of the books being reviewed.

#7 (1984). Editors: Peter Balakian and Bruce Smith.
POB 5000, Colgate University, Hamilton, NY 13346. $9 for
2 yrs. $17 for 4.

GRAHAM HOUSE REVIEW has had almost a decade to get
its act together. Judging from this issue, it fumbles
and stumbles along and already boasts liver spots.
Evidence of its failure to age gracefully is its mix of
tame poets with reputations and those without--here
Madeline DeFrees and Jon Silkin adorn the pages, the
flotsam riding over the jetsam. There is also a
fashionable section of translations (except for those by
Jascha Kessler these are tepid), and a pallid
interview--here, of a fine, relatively unknown poet John
Wheatcroft, a long-term professor at Bucknell. Like
most interviews, this one has too many hollow-spots.
Why don't these mags simply devote such wasted pages to
more poems by the interviewee? Wheatcroft is a
discovery--I had not known his work. Three poems (plus
one inserted into the interview) are pretty slim
pickings. I hungered for more.

That the issue is dedicated to Richard Hugo's
memory hints at the sort of poems the editors favor:
local types--drunks, bakers, hunchbacks, and family
members, all written up by poets who don't seem to have
read much, and employ mediocre Writing Program devices,
among them the Deep Image, and the First-Person Ego
Mode. De Frees, in her elegy for Hugo, remembers that
Hugo liked "pretending not to read." I fear that hordes
of young admirers have taken him at his word.

Here's Gary Fincke on making bread--the baker has
his "hands busy inside / The rising, dependent dough."
For good measure (a dollop of Hugo-esque clabber),
there's a drunk who "sugar-dreamed his way / Toward
morning." Also, we face the hoary father-son poem. One
of these, by Judson Mitcham, includes these woefully
spavined lines:
                    Whatever it is
you have searched for eludes you yet.
Your own light and the light I read by both
          guide you.
A sleepwalker also once, I know those lights,
how certainty will fade toward certainty. Son,
come sit with me.

On the positive side, Laurie Blauner writes
superbly of a daughter-father relationship. She doesn't

swamp her lines with clumsy literary   dreck, dull
prepositional phrases that limp along like snakes with
their backs broken. Incest seems to be the theme: and
the girl grown is still trapped by her father, in
memories that both pain and give pleasure: "I cannot
leave the sound of your breath lifting to a scar of
light...." When she was fifteen, her mother died,
apparently in a car-wreck, "like a moth trapped in a
lamp." Then her father came to her bed:

> That night the dogwood catching porchlight in
>   its thin network of life
> was a woman's smooth fingers testing the weight
>   of pearls.
> The architect of the heart is memory. I
>   touched lips and limbs so like my own.

This is a first-rate blend of nature images and passion,
with the awe and wonder of discovery. Blauner does not
flag: the closing stanza is potent, subtle, and strange:

> The thin fan of bones in my hands are Mama's.
> They lead like rivulets to the heart she wanted
>   to offer
> to an acceptable beau. Honeysuckle roses
>   eclipse my breasts.
> I cannot grow away from you. This night's
>   moonlight lies against my bones
> to listen, to hold the shape of my body
>   in its light.
> You call me your ghost. A still wind
>   rests in my hands.

You'll also find a healthy spread of Hugo-inspired
flora and fauna, and accounts of the seasons, lead up to
by utterly slack opening lines, again in Hugo's manner.
The solipsistic "I" is a must. As crackers are to
cheese, so I is to this poem. Robert Gibb opens "March"
this way:

> If I were good enough,
> Patient enough, and attentive,
> I would be able to tell you
> Everything I've seen today--
> . . .
> The loving minutia of a world
> Turning into spring.

Nothing seems felt. The props are vapid and commonplace.
Later, after remarking on "the face of your startling
presence," Gibb throws in snow nudging down "its bank";
a turtle "clacking over stones;" and geese, skunk
cabbage, crocus sprouts, and some "tiny berries" he

can't name. The final stanza reveals the malady well:
the phony predictable literary phrases ("an ascension of
days") followed by the one breath of originality in the
poem:

> I want to tell you how nothing
> Changes except in particulars,
> How March is an ascension
> Of days, and a thaw I've felt
> Like a tongue licking me clean.

You'll also find a good spread of metaphysics here.
One of the featured poets, Cleopatra Mathis, a teacher
at Dartmouth, inspired by William Blake, creates a
cartoonish God, filled with "wonder and regret" over
Adam. In a good professorial stroke (numerous poems
here have allusions to moments from famous poems taught
in Surveys of Literature classes: Yeats is a big
favorite), Mathis wrenches John Donne's famous compass
image: God's creation of Adam leads to a speculation
about his leg:

> God means that leg as tree
> rooted to one place, as the other will want
> always to carry him away
> on feet which are the boniest of fish.

God, who "needs no muscle," is "two arms and a face,"
has "one gorgeous pair of wings," and is Adam's "lover."
As he opens "the flower of Adam's face" (I like this)
God "is blind with wonder/and regret." The remainder of
Mathis' poems deal with assorted Big Themes, and not
particularly well. In the Hugo tradition, she immerses
herself in weather. In "Night Storm" she's out in the
snow, facing up to "the pearls" of her "inadequacy."
She can't see much in the blizzard--but she keeps the
icicles from forming in her mind by meditating on earth
and life in general (write me, dear reader, if you know
how her gray hat gets into the scene):

> ...for everything I've tried to believe in,
> this earth as choice, not an accident
> that I happen to see its losses, its arbitrary
>   returns.
> What can I count on in this blindness
> flying against my face, what can I distinguish
> except the gray hat swept into the fury
> that goes on transforming?

She can be sentimental along with the best of them--and
this was one of Hugo's failings: a babe's breath has
"tiny white flowers," a cat's yawn is a "pink-tongued
sigh." In this passage, I can't tell whether her fists,

or the chest she presses, is ovate:

                    I hold my two fists
          against the middle of your chest,
          the size of my own heart, the shape of an egg.
          And in the egg, the filled cell
          dividing, the pull and release.

Please understand, I am not opposed to eggs, whether they appear in spring, summer, or winter, or whether they are hidden in God's mustache--what bothers me is writing (about eggs or anything else) that seems ill-conceived. Robert Phillips supplies yet another God/Adam poem, one of no particular distinction.

     Madeline DeFrees, Director of the Writing Program at the University of Massachusetts, rings in with five poems at the most prestigious position in the journal, the head. (Wheatcroft occupies that other prestigious spot, the tail). DeFrees writes chattily of Richard Hugo and of her trip to Greece--one sensitive woman's experience kissed by many Yeatsian phrases: "the whitening shore," "a human presence," "the big dreamfish" Yeats and Hugo "were after"). She loves journalese beginnings: "You told me once where we / were serious," "Feeling nervous, out of place and halfway through / the Greek orthodox Sunday service," "Halfway up the mountain." The elegy to Hugo is effective, if slack. DeFrees admires the dead poet's maleness: he loved jack salmon, sea gulls, starfish, and pretended not to like reading books. He liked hard-drinking workingmen and cement mixers.

     A trap for most elegiasts, which DeFrees does not avoid, is the fiction that the departed one doesn't know what's happened since he died--the survivor must fill in the news. This pitch is cloying: if Hugo dead can hear a living DeFrees, why isn't he capable of seeing what's happening to her in Greece? Do souls in Heaven (if that's where Hugo is?) have ears but no eyes? Even if he were like Cleopatra Mathis's God, with two arms and a face, he should still be able to see. The result of this fictioneering is an off-putting sentimentality. DeFrees' poem reaches its nadir at the end, in chatter rather than felt emotion. She imagines Hugo as a coat wrapped about her in "grey / weather." His voice, she promises him, will be "strong" in her ear, "falling like these coastal rains / to fill the reservoir or float the Big Sky / home, riding your favorite thermals." I'm glad thermals refers to clouds and not to underwear.

     While I do not doubt the authenticity of DeFrees' Greek experiences, I suspect her flagging energies: she seems caught between the Snapshot Poem (they used to be called the Fulbright Poem, or the Academic Abroad Poem), her need to rift the writing with easy metaphysical speculations ("I learned to wait / on the dead. Light the candle one more time."), and ludicrous phrases dealing little deaths to otherwise felt moments. In a Greek Orthodox church (She's gone to the men's side.) the priest is "ensconced in a separate / altitude." This sits like stale almonds on a collapsed cake. Nor are things freshened up by easy references to Henry Miller, Yeats, Andrew Marvell, Brueghel, and Francis Thompson fleeing that Hound of Heaven. Here's DeFrees: "Of course I fled: through cobbled porticoes, weed, / brambles, rock, to a dead-end / precipice." Further, monotonous cadences abound, the result, I think of her fondness for certain padded phrases, adverbial, adjectival, nominative, and prepositional: "I knew I didn't belong," "I wanted to see/the gift-shop nun," white-washed cell walls "expected to impress / remind me of the past, mean something else / to me...."

Her "Gallery of the Sarcophagi: Heraklion Museum" is good enough to invalidate nearly all of my carpings. She has a delicious sense of humor, and swings through her DON JUAN, ottava rima stanzas like a twentieth-century Lady Hesther Stanhope masquerading as Byron. She needs a bath:

> Worse luck. The first bathtubs I've found
>   in Crete
> and both in use by nice clean skeletons,
> their knees drawn up, their feet deliberate
> as a will.

She engages in a brief, funny meditation on those recumbent bones, and concludes with this couplet:

> Call the museum guard, evict the squatter.
> Impound the cameras and bring on the water.

She needs to use her wits, she writes, to help the "mislaid" dead reach eternity:

> Sometimes the body's laid out like a hero
> sandwich. At others, neatly wrapped in pit
>   or grotto.
> The best-dressed corpses in the west since Nero
> prefer to make the journey obbligato,
> fall on a word, a sword, the instant zero
> ground approaches--or back upon a motto:
> Abandon soap, all ye who enter here.
> No sheets, no shoes, no service. Try our bier!

John Wheatcroft, in his interview, sees American

poetry diverging two ways--via Whitman (the secular and expansive) and Dickinson (the sacramental and the traditional). His own poems are far more in the spirit of the latter than the former. Other influences are Vaughan, Herbert, and Donne. He sees his work (and himself) quite modestly "as an expendable anachronism." He feels few ties with "a great deal of verse that is being written today," and finds "faddism" horrifying. He avoids most contemporaries, he says, because he doesn't want to be influenced by what they are writing. He does have a few good words for Hugo and for Kinnell; and he has some superficial, and quite untrue, remarks to make of Alfred Lord Tennyson, clichès that any self-respecting Victorian Specialist (I am one) will loathe: Tennyson found all that "nice order and harmony in things" and made poems with all "the right sounds and the rhymes all fall in the right place." That's stupid. Any careful reading of IN MEMORIAM and MAUD will show how thoroughly aware Tennyson was of his "imperfect universe"--and his poetry reflects it.

When you read Wheatcroft's poems, you'll conclude that he is as well-shaped as he thinks Tennyson is, without anything to match the originality of Tennyson's music or themes. Yet, Wheatcroft's obligatory father/son poem, "Runagate" is lean and touching: he's still guilty over abandoning the Protestant ideals (or drastically modifying them) of his preacher father. He's a child of six again, in his pew--which resembles a bath:

> Slowly I grow calm. The water turns
> lukewarm as the church at Laodicea.
> I feel so limp, were some imp to pull the plug
> I'd slither down the drain, leaving as
> last will and testament, a ring of dirt.

I love his "Village Church, Yorkshire." He's fresh and imaginative in his bringing to life a sense of the Medieval builders of the church, which now lies utterly abandoned:

> They had so much to doubt, those builders:
> surviving winter, hunger, Black Death,
> axes and fire brands wielded by giants with red
> or blonde beards and flowing manes; gaining
> access to water the beaver-like monks
> at Rievaulx were diverting eastward,
>   down the valley;
> the gentleness of the fist inside
> the gauntlet of de Mowbray's henchmen....

The old church, a withered "fig tree" now has padlocks, the oak portals are split, and wire mesh protects its

windows "like a hauberk." Like the old church,
Wheatcroft is himself "a tare in a croft of wheat." "I
belong here," he says.

I regret not being able to provide a more positive
reading of GRAHAM HOUSE REVIEW. It suffers from the
maladies of a host of inept literary journals around the
country--there's no daring in selecting poets (although
their blurb boasts that they publish "the best in
contemporary poetry"), nothing memorable in either
layout or design, and the writing is suffocatingly
limited to Big Themes, cosy moments from nature, and
much solipsistic use of the first person, after the
manner of the poets they've featured: Dave Smith, David
Wagoner, Michael Harper, and Stanley Moss.

GRAND STREET

Vol. 3: No. 3 (Spring 1984). Editor: Ben Sonnenberg.
50 Riverside Drive, New York, NY 10024. Quarterly. $14
per year.

This fat, prestigious-looking journal is one of the
most professional around. This issue features nine
poets, nine fiction writers, a fascinating historical
piece by Nora Sayre on the Cambridge Poets' Theater in
the 'fifties, and a brainy piece on philosophy and
literature by Arthur C. Danto. GRAND STREET has no
stated academic connections, is set up as a not-for-
profit venture, and exists on NEA and New York State
Council on the Arts grants, and on "generous donors."

The drift of the journal is indeed grand. If you
are not published by a trade house or have never
appeared in THE NEW YORKER or THE NATION your chances
here are almost nil. Only one poet, Susan Stein (she
lives in New York City) appears in print for the first
time. The other poets have books either by or

forthcoming from Atheneum, Ecco, Faber and Faber, Knopf, Houghton Mifflin, Dragon Gate, and Sheep Meadow. The latter two may sound like small presses--but don't be fooled. GRAND STREET is a pretty closed organ, antediluvean, not designed for risks.

Yet, the poetry is worth a read. Donald Finkel (Atheneum; Washington University) glosses up the hairy issue of abortion with a reference to beggars in ancient Troy with much sibillance. Once we pass the "writing," we find a nicely angry poem--Finkel is against the anti-abortionists. In "Salisbury Cathedral from the Bishop's Ground," inspired by John Constable, Finkel once again spins beautiful sounds ("they wrought the transmutations of lead, / by precipitation.") The Cathedral was built so that "Constable's cows might safely graze / and meek grass turn to clotted cream."

Sandra McPherson (Ecco Press, Oregon Writers' Workshop) is more ambitious than Finkel. She's into hip feminist issues--the first poem is stimulated by a man who denies that 95.65 of single-parent households in Oregon are headed by women. The poem meanders. McPherson has retreated to an Idaho motel, aching to stop the flow of words in her life. She considers borrowing from the Icelandic: "a strong-toothed language with three-legged words/ And hard-shinned sentences." There's so much talk! She visits infant graves in a Pocatello cemetery, and considers the woeful conditions many women face, alone. There's a sardonic, moving close:

> I imagine, estimating by these green-glossed,
> Unmoving grave-lanes,
> Some mothers do get off relief:
> For Twins Jeanette and Emma, Infant Joe and
>   Baby Cain--
> Perpetual child care.

"Ledge" is in a different mode--the lines are much shorter, the moments from nature delicate and sure. Any return to water (McPherson bathes in a mountain lake) automatically generates easy motifs of regeneration, purification, restoration. McPherson avoids the traps.

The less said about Craig Raine the better. His line-breaks may delight Faber and Faber, but they don't amuse me. They interfere with meaning, and for no apparent reason other than showing off. He writes a fashionable two-line stanza--one of the easiest of all unrhymed forms, and he is often coy and pretentious. Here is one of his efforts at Significance: "He has deduced that objects // need love because they are lonely. / Everything touches something else. // Being is lost if the law is broken." Much of his writing seems automatic. This is woeful: "And the boy belongs to her / who drives his toast // round a difficult bend / with multiplied lips, / or settles to sleep / by sipping his thumb." Moments are frequently hilarious (by design?): "angular buttocks / crusted with cradle cap"; asthma-tortured trout; a grand piano with "a dangerous fin...."

David St. John (Houghton Mifflin, Johns Hopkins) writes up a bland reminiscence of his boyhood. He walks with his aunt through Sausalito, sees a girl holding a blank writing tablet, staring out at the Pacific. His aunt "shrugged & said Too bad No inspiration." Later, they pass a coffee shop, and, guess what, Lenny Bruce winks at young St. John. That makes his day. St. John doesn't do much with it though, copping out with an easy tear-jerk. He glances back to see Bruce talking to some woman. She's laughing hard: "...pretty soon she was almost / Bent over almost crying I think crying."

Linda Gregerson (Dragon's Gate, Poetry, Parnassus) adopts another fashionable easy form, the free verse quatrain. The lines are mostly three-stress, with an occasional four-stress line thrown in. She writes in homage of St. Agatha, whom she sets up as a patron saint of women barren in both womb and breast, and those who must hire themselves out as wet-nurses. The subject is provocative. Alas, Gregerson seldom hits the mark-- perhaps because her rhythms are clumpers--there's little real grace; and the Saint's descent into slang seems cute. Yet, there are some fine touches--Agatha's gown "stiff with embroidery" resembles the gowns "the wounded" wear in heaven, gowns "that teach them the leverage // of pain."

Grace Schulman (Sheep Meadow), writes of going to the doctor for heart palpitations. The patient is hooked up to various electronic machines. Those stanzas interweave with couplets (often with a skillful turn in the manner of Edna St. Vincent Millay) of nature, music, and meditation. The final stanza fuses the medical matter with the Millay matter:

> Radar angel, what of the hawk's sway,
> the bulrush, marigolds, the heron's cry,
> of earth's erratic lights and shadows? There
> let your needle calculate disorder.

GYPSY: DIE SYMPATHISCHE ALTERNATIVE

(1984). Editors: Belinda Subraman and S. Ramnath. % Tom
Burgarner, 105 Elledge Mill Road, North Wilkesboro, NC
28659 or VERGIN PRESS, Kappelbergsteig 29, 8540
Schwabach, West Germany(until June 1985). $4 per copy.

GYPSY bills itself as "an energetic, independent
and international look at the literary arts." It is
randy, and eschews what the editors condemn as "sissy
language poetry." Several poets who turn up here, also
write for BOGG, NORTHERN PLEASURE, and GARGOYLE: Ron
Androla (he provides the cover collage), Hugh Fox,
Gerald Dorset, Todd Moore, Gerald Locklin, and, for good
measure, Charles Bukowski. A passel of United Kingdom
poets swirl among the Americans.

Kenneth Sutherland sets the randy tone, the
unsissified language. His grammar is careless: "I wonder
who she's thinking of?" Is his sweetie worth his
attention? He doubts her honesty, and wonders why she
cries. The conclusion? She seems to have given him a
social disease: "I wonder / why / it hurts / when I /
piss." Charles Bukowski and Gerald Locklin do the
predictable: as Bukowski drinks wine a fly sails into
his mouth. He pours a new drink, observes the fly still
squirming in the ashtray: "there we were / a wino fly
and a wino man / at 1:30 a.m." He hears a second fly
buzzing in to join the party:

        well, I could be drinking with
        things that can't
        fly
        either with body
        or
        any other
        way.
        and you can't
        spit them
        out.

Emily Dickinson Bukowski is not!

In "Funny," Bukowski further fills us in on kinds
of women he's known: one laughed when he was serious,

calling him "the funniest man."   When he tried to be
funny, she missed the point.   When they "seperated"
(sic) he hooks up with another broad who was into her
own thing, laughing along with the laugh track on the
TV.   Buk finally figures it out, in a nice little life-
motto:

       the truth is the funniest thing
       around
       because you seldom ever hear
       it
       and when you do
       it astonishes you into
       laughter.

Is Bukowski, as he ages, turning into the Martin
Farquahr Tupper of the age?

     Gerald Locklin has run out of money.   Rooting for
payday, he observes, is "rooting" for his own death.

     Some of the poems take proletarian turns.   Kevin
Sweeney puts down a "semi-famous writer" and a fan he
sees in a Maine resort island supermarket:

          HE WORE tight shorts
       a T-shirt that said "Racquetball Club,"
       blue & gold running shoes,
       off-white sweat socks;
       his thighs were long, thin, tanned,
       his hair and moustache clipped....

He's met by a "tennis-dressed woman / from the WASP side
of the island."   She's cool, says "beef for the
stroganoff," and doesn't like New York.   A "fat sullen
clerk" ain't impressed: she throws Sweeney a "mean /
freckled look" and says: "I can take you over here."   Us
proles must hang together!   The rich make us puke.

     George Cairncross's cartoonish saga of an English
prole is wierdly touching.   Harry is blessed with six
toes on his left foot, has fifty million hairs on his
head, and a cupboard filled with empty Vodka bottles. An
index finger on which six parakeets can perch, and a
huge collection of bottle tops.   That he's never been to
tea at the palace, or found his name on the Honours
list, doesn't matter: last week a tree felled him, in
Oldham.

     The uneasiness implicit behind these verses burbles
forth in Tom House's "Post Modern Graffiti." His poem
reads like a cut-up freshman composition: the ideas are
not subtle. Art has become "the province / of misfits
and ne'er do wells" who won't accept prosperity.   House

47

adopts the conservative, Reaganesque voice: these souls
are "infantile" in spreading their "discontent /
negativity / and frustrated selves." The warning?
"Prosperity" appears "freer than art." We are "close"
to "pissing it all away."

    Kurt Nimmo places himself on a riverbank opposite a
polluted city. Trees are "very tired." When a girl
climbs into a "tired" tree and wants her picture
snapped, Nimmo thinks about all the chemicals in the
river, and how "organic fibers" have been "murdered."

    In the most entertaining piece, "Topigal Subject,"
John Taylor riffs on pigs. Some of his puns are
delicious: viz., "What is called a pig in England is
called a sow in Penury." "What kind of fundamental tail
has a pig really got?" "Like religion snort language is
a powerful unifying and dividing force."

    The problem with GYPSY is that the editors opt for
one-take poems, with few exceptions: Gerald Dorset's
"Eros Revisited" and Deborah Seyler's "Interstate."
And the editing is careless: "definate" for "definite",
and "seperated" for "separated." I want to like GYPSY,
but fear that it falls into a self-made trap: iconoclasm
is fine--for it to succeed, though, it has to provide
readers with artistry, sensitivity, and some fresh
ideas. There should be one poem, at least, you would
like to be kissed by. One of the featured poets, Jim
Haynes offers this sophomoric advice:

    "If you feel the world needs more smiles, smile
more. If you like to see clean streets and fields,
don't litter. In fact, pick up litter when you see it.
Be an example. Care. If you have more than enough,
share with others. Even if you don't have enough, share
anyway. // Because of everything and in spite of
everything, life is!"

Can he be serious? Is this hippie pablum, derived from
the sixties? GYPSY, at least in this number, waffles
around.

IRONWOOD

#21(1983). Editor: Michael Cuddihy. Box 40907, Tucson,
AZ 85717. Twice yearly. $6 per year, individuals;
$6.50 institutions.

> "This water is full of dogs."
> > --Laura Mullen

"We felt bored / And at the same time like screaming
Biblical phrases..."
> --Robert Pinsky

> "Pitiless verse? A few words tuned
> And tuned and tuned and tuned."
> > --Wallace Stevens, "Gallant Chateau"

i

    Some 40 poets are represented here, quite a
sizeable cabbage for those interested in a lot of bulk
for their money. The format is professional and glossy,
almost slick. Poems are beautifully displayed, with
lots of white space--no marks of the residual earth.
They're sanitized, complete with plenty of saran wrap.

    What makes this issue of IRONWOOD so boring? Be
advised, poets thinking of submitting work here. It
helps if you are currently in one of the better-known
Writing Programs or on a Literature faculty. It helps
to have Guggenheims. Useful also is your having
appeared before in IRONWOOD, either in the magazine
itself or in an IRONWOOD book or chapbook. Having
books from the Wesleyan or Copper Canyon presses, or in
the National Poetry Series, helps. While modest space
is allowed young poets appearing in print for the first
time (these seem to come from the "better" Writing
Programs and were probably ushered forth by their
mentors, who also are IRONWOOD poets), the featured
authors are in the 30-45 age range. Finally, it helps if
you have appeared in APR, SALMAGUNDI, THE SOUTHERN
POETRY REVIEW, POETRY NORTHWEST, THE SENECA REVIEW, THE
GEORGIA REVIEW, or POETRY. None of these mags is
reknowned for imagination or energy (see my first PETERS
BLACK AND BLUE GUIDE, Cherry Valley Editions). As for
topics--if you write about handicapped or senile
parents, fathers teaching sons to be men, cats or cows
or bears and pastoral living, walks on beaches,
various genteel sexual rites-of-passage you'll be on
track, ploughing IRONWOOD furrows.

48

ii

Of the celebrities (and they are numerous) Mary Oliver writes the best. With enviable precision her "Beethoven" explores frustrations and pain. There is an old-fashioned, Emersonian principle of "compensation" at work. If an arm withers the other arm strengthens, enabling us to get on with our lives. There is often a glory to be seen, as "wrong" comes not to hurt at all and "shines like a new moon." Beethoven is her model: she imagines him an insomniac, "stumbling through the dust and crumpled papers," settling himself at the piano, "inking in rapidly note after note after note." Her second poem, "On the Plains," while less well-realized (there's confusion as to whether the bear is shot by a hunter dressed as a bear, or whether hunter or bear are present at all, has vapid moments: the rivers and all the "grains of the earth" endlessly reassemble "ev erything." And this coy observation: as the astute bear falls "he remembers the responsible circle." IRONWOOD poets have a penchant for stepping into animal brains as easily as they enter their bathrooms.

After Oliver, IRONWOOD, alas, speeds down hill. Laura Mullen, who was awarded the mag's Frank Stanford prize of $500 "for the strongest group of four or more poems," writes this way: She loves the splayed line, and wrenches her poem's centipedinous legs at odd angles from its exo-skeleton. Dull, lingering phrases, border on being clichès: "to let go gracefully," "a little worn at the edges," "formalities we were brought up to appreciate." When she is conceptual, or philosophical, like most of her cohorts in IRONWOOD 21, she creaks. The ocean throws its "clockworks" up onto a "dry shore," occasioning this vapid Rilkean sentiment: "You remember the life you left here." It's enough to make one wish Rilke had never written that sonnet to Apollo's torso. In "Broken Pantoum For Three Voices" she takes a cue, apparently from Virginia Woolf, fills her pockets with stones, and walks into the sea. Stones dragging along through the waves make her jaw ache. Her "Narcissus" opens with a calculated flatness (the italics are mine):

> And everything there was the color of rain.
> It rained all the time there.
> And everythig
> took on the same heron, redwood...

Why don't poets know what any amateur actor knows? You begin your speech with an attack, ie., some energy, you don't mumble, whisper, or lull? In Mullen's 4th prize-winning poem, "Glass of Water," she takes one of the least interesting of all still-life subjects, a glass of water. Things do liven up--she's in an anatomy lab. An old woman's corpse is dumped out of a plastic bag. Mullen steps back and makes a harsh experience pretty: the dried body has a "crazy quilt of skin," all "scraps and patches" over it. Then, this non-sequitur occurs: Mullen limns the old woman's "sex," for "it too had turned / to rock." Why doesn't she say "genitals"--is that too clinical? Not pretty enough for the editors of IRONWOOD? She behaves in good workshop fashion (if you mention the gun/glass in line 1, it has to go off, or be gurgled down by the end) she picks up the glass and drinks. A heavy Lit. Interp. Class communion metaphor?

Another master of the splayed line is <u>Thomas Centolella</u>, with these contributions: "the pleasure of speaking"--which he repeats; "the matrix of chance," "earnest talk of weather," "the denser sweat of human effort." My complaint is that piling these phrases ("of"s stand like raisins in stale suet) deprives the poem of swiftness, elan, thrust--all qualities, it seems to me, a good poem should have. If your reader nods, you've failed.

<u>James Baker Hall</u> wins $100 for more "strong" poems. He's a bit more gifted than Mullen, although he shows he can write as badly as she does. "Remembering" opens this way:

> When the sun reaches the flat rock
> on which the cat sleeps
> the heat dreams her.

Is this a mistake? How does heat "dream?" Is "her" the cat? a lover standing off to the side?   There is one fine observation: Hall's pussy draws her leg slowly after her as she enters the shadow of a tree. But Hall can't let a good thing go, and proceeds to squeeze the life out of it by turning cerebral: cat seems aware that "her condition" is "to change shape with every move." Cows as well as cats are prescient. Like the heat earlier, cows standing in water "dreaming themselves," remember more and more "the blacker they become." Hall assumes a Robert <u>Frostian</u> stance (lots of IRONWOOD poets do), alert for impulses from a vernal wood, pastures, and firkins. This passeth for profundity:

> The older a place is
> the more ways it has
> not to move.

One discerns Frost's breath here as a shibboleth or verity, viz., "home is the place where when you go they have to take you in," or however that runs. While Frost had style, Hall merely sounds pompous and wields his line breaks in the ugliest manner possible.

Linda Gregg (featured in IRONWOOD 14, and a Guggenheim Fellow), Michael Burkard, and Susan Mitchell (a Wesleyan poet) are typical of many poets who embroider the trivia of their lives, waving aloft numerous Ego Banners. Mitchell is the worst of this trio. When she takes refuge in a cave during a rainstorm (Oh, where is Dido? Where is Aeneas?), she finds BOONE (for Daniel Boone) carved into the rock (which she informs us is "hard"). As she parades herself about inside her solipsistic cave, grass, as it stretches to the west starts to gain speed "like an animal running for the sheer / joy of running...." That seems quite impossible. The simile flops on its face. She mindlessly zooms ahead and imagines Boone trapping, each of his traps "biting deeper / into the green absence of prairie." (Note the fancy abstraction. IRONWOOD poets are shamelessly addicted to them). And she continues: "I lay there thinking," "I listened to the wind," I prayed / to be unremembered as the dirt."

Burkard loves enervated abstractions: "aloneness," "emptiness." The first eight lines of "Single White Shape" contain twelve "I," or "my/myself" phrases:

On a day like today
I feel like an imitation of one of my own poems.
I try to read others, I try to walk, but I have
    trouble
and my head feels like one hundred days.
And I think of myself, sitting in this building,
yesterday and last night, and I think of myself
sitting in this building today and tonight
and I recognize no one. I don't hear anything....

Some of his effects are ludicruous. In "Open Boat" he finger-paints a circle and opines: "The sea / reports to the field, / where the trees are." Ugh.

Jim Burbank's generous chunk of Rio Grande Breaks seems promising. He writes Creeleyesque lines, yet eschews compact writing, rolling out his poem-crust to the thinnest of doughs. He parades his superficial knowledge: mountains hold minerals, precious stones, and crystals. He requires several lines to tell us this. He is meditative, and like most of these poets, seems stuck back there in Philosophy I, or in a bad course on the reflections of Eliot, Stevens, and Frost. "Time passes," we are informed. Generations of men have long since vanished. Cities are horrible. There are unsubtle echoes of Wordsworth's "getting and spending" ("in the drone of / buying and selling"); bad <u>Hamlet</u> : "perchance to dream" (for we come / to sleep / only to dream"); bad GENESIS ("all creatures who / fly run or creep"); and bad Omar Khayyam ("like water / we change.") My quarrel is not with Burbank so much as it is with journals like IRONWOOD and ill-formed poets in MFA workshops who encourage these tender folk to regard themselves as their own <u>Aristotle</u> or <u>Emmanuel Kant</u>. What a disservice to poetry!

One of of the best-known of IRONWOOD's celebrity poets is <u>Robert Pinsky</u>, who supplies a poem "The Unseen." The title should prepare us immediately for some chintzy intellectualization. And we get it. Despite a flicker of energy at the end, the poem lacks any real emotion. It is "writing" in a bad sense--the piece is self-consciously designed in triplet stanzas, much as a miser might arrange all his guineas into piles of three. The rhymes seem fashioned rather than felt (a riff on <u>air</u> runs throughout the first four stanzas. And the fancy diction! Warmed over <u>Keats</u>? <u>Shelley</u> splattering the guests at Crotchet Castle? Here are some of the worst phrases: "Menu of immensities." "A formal, dwindled feeling." "The single power of invisibility." Pinsky loads in fancy, cinematic violence, flushing (his word) it away in "fire and blood" as he drifts off to sleep. Snore. Snore. Is it any reason why students admiring Pinsky and similar masters write as badly as they do?

Another poet who helps create poets via his NORTHEAST magazine and Juniper Press books is <u>John Judson</u>. His "Dunker's Island" commemorates a late-adolescent sex-rite. A set of friends, on graduating, hire a slut and take her to an island where she is gang-banged. Sounds promising? It's thoroughly genteel. The poet and his friend Mitch hide outside and wait below a window, listening to the "mumbles and thumps." Now, twenty years later, Judson looks back and opines that what was going on grew "sour with light...." That's a fancy step for dancing around one of the hoariest of all verse clichés: <u>Homer's</u> rosy-fingered dawn. If Judson had driven deeper into his sexual fears we might have had a terrific poem. As it is, the event is a cliché--all boys have similar tales to tell.

IRONWOOD also features a cluster of pretty dismal family poems. <u>Stephen Dunning</u> wipes the feces off his mother's "backside"--she's senile, it appears. He ruminates utterly predictable thoughts. <u>Leslie Wolf</u> commemorates an apparently blind father attacked by bees. Before the tragedy occurs, the poet sits at his dad's desk and props his feet up, remarking on "the glassed pose" of family pictures spread out before him.

David Baker has a father gut a catfish for a sensitive son. There's some vivid stuff, but at the end Baker zooms in on the fish's heart, which the "sad boy" senses as his own. Ann Neelon writes of her "Mama," in the voice of a Senagalese woman. Neelon was in the Peace Corps in Senegal. Her poem is effective at the close, but is terrible before that. Her point of view as a foetus just doesn't come off; it's labored.

Jane Miller thrusts several pages of writing over the page in William Carlos Williams' late manner. Since she is to appear in the National Poetry Series (to date not impressive for its originality) some comment is in order. I like her use of the only gross four-letter word in the whole magazine: "o shit," she exclaims, "foul // glue of resin, dew, sap, steam." She has all the flaws I've complained of in other poets here--and she parades them with an irritating smugness. The nadir is this: "I am / in my thirties now where I might be enjoying / labor, independence, travel." Again, there are tame echoes of Frost: "I've come to love only what I have to do." There are the trite profundities: "I've come to love the light." She dotes on the pathetic fallacy, and here gives flowers an embarrassing prescience: "The daisies the iris called upon so often so kind...." She can be sleazily didactic: "Tenderness in distance // is the death in distance / shared." This comes off as a tepid Pythagorean theorem for life. Here is another: "Even among the few we know / how many we are." And just try reading this either for rhythm or sense:

> funny Southern vowels elegy to
> part of me knows you....

Miller seems to have dropped cut-up words on her carpet, then pasted them on the page without caring much about either syntax or sense. And there are unintentionally humorous touches, viz., spring birds return to the farm dropping the "first manure" of the season. I simply cannot imagine that so ill-formed a writer will appear in the National Poetry Series. The fact says much about the general indifference of editors and publishers, yes, to quality. IRONWOOD is symptomatic; it is not the only source of our leprosy.

In fairness, there are a few good poems. I have already mentioned Mary Oliver's. Others are by Michael Palmer (his is delicious, almost a playlet, and has real brains); Jorie Graham (I've seen inept work by her in other places, but this poem is good); and Yusef Komunhakaa. This minority though doesn't begin to justify the dreck--go thumb your bibles for good phrases to scream.

MAGAZINE

Vol XIV:No. 2(Spring 1984).   Editor: Jocelyn Fisher.
Managing Editor: Alexandra Garrett.   Beyond Baroque
Foundation, POB 806, Venice, CA 90291. $7 for 6 issues.

Among regional cultural efforts, Beyond Baroque Foundation is unique.   Southern California writers and artists benefit greatly by the Foundation's varied activities.   The Literary/Arts Center Bookstore is the only place in the region one can purchase literary journals and small press books. The library is well-stocked, and is much used by borrowers. The Gallery hosts art exhibitions, and on-going writing workshops are the oldest in Southern California.   There is an exciting Reading/Performance series, with a good mix of East and West Coast poets(with stops in between).   Young talents are preferred to older ones, although established writers are as varied as John Logan, Peter Schjeldahl, Paul Metcalf, James Broughton, and Edward Field.   Beyond Baroque also has a Print Center, where, for a minimal fee, writers and fledgling publishers are instructed in the vagaries of typesetting, book-design, and lay-out.   I understand that there is no other bargain like it in the country.   The Berkeley Print Center, once competitive, is now apparently on a par with commerical print-shops.   The crown jewel of Beyond Baroque activities is MAGAZINE, which has seen many transformations since it's founding by George Drury Smith fifteen years ago.

MAGAZINE has appeared in its current news-print format for two years now, and each issue gets better-- the writing is not as thoroughly Los Angeles and street- poet centered as it once was.   More poets from elsewhere, particularly from the East, appear; and the reviews, since Tom Clark is aboard, are iconoclastic.
Los Angeles poet Lori Cohen celebrates her far-out family--they seemed to go for out-of-body experiences shot through with light waves.   Spring comes to Los Angeles as an intensification of the "hysteria" already there. A bit freakier is Cohen's monologue, "Antigone's Last Day." Shades of Patti Smith doing her Rimbaud-riff do their funky jig behind this one:

It's silly: an obvious act
knocks everyone over. A veil,
real linen, is my floor,

54

my net.
These walls, buried rock
emit an augury pulse,
a biased blip-blip I feel
through my sandals.
It's Haemon,
his boots forcing dust in.
His sword chisels the face off
a rock. The eyes ascend first:
new motes I'm happy to lead
through this ardent countryside.

Paul Hoover (he edits OINK in Chicago) contributes an
ode "In Praise of Boredom":

Life should be so average a pink
clothes hamper is the highlight of
the day. We shiver to imagine
grandmother's first plane ride

. . . .
Can't things be usual ever, not
the prince with his thrilling smile
but the frog with its level gaze?
Please, a glass of water, a simple glass
of water! But already it's too exciting.

Hoover's "Response To A Questionaire For a Twentieth
High School Reunion" is also in the pop mode. He won't
be going to the reunion:

but I wish you all the best.
Last week, if you must know,
I shaved off the moustache I'd had
for fourteen years. My lips had
gotten thinner. Otherwise, it's me.

His "At the Music Box" is drenched with old film
nostalgia dear to LA readers and writers--some of them
are film and TV actors. He likes tacky experience
covered in cobwebs:

On screen, an ancient print
of Wuthering Heights barely smothers light.
Even the shadows gleam at the edge; then,
to my delight, the projectionist's giant
hand removes a nest of lint and dust
that had gathered on the lens. What is
Heathcliff doing, mucking about in the
heather, filling his arms with Cathy?
. . . .   Cathy dies
at the window while silly Heathcliff
holds her, then two ghosts holding hands
walks into the sunset like all the movies
then: Glenn Ford in the Army, Bill Holden....

It's a wonderful poem, as zany and hip as an old plastic jukebox swimming in colored light.

Gerald Locklin tries to snag us with this attention-getting title, "I sure as fuck hope he's not right." "He" is Edward Field, one of the three living poets Locklin most respects, so he tells us. This leads to Locklin's grandmother, which leads to another poem about driving up Mt. Baldy with a two-year old and a blue nun--a Used Kleenex Mysticism/Social Commentary poem poured into one of Locklin's old wine-skins: the only poetry left in a landscape now smothered with tract homes is in the street names. The "blue nun" opines that "it's nice that the chicanos / have mt. baldy to drive up to." Holly Prado continues to write in the intimate personal mode she has made her trademark: she celebrates her lover, poet/actor Harry Northup, and writes sensitively of a dead mother:

> I want to bury you again
> where you belong
> not in the city where you never lived
> where you only died in unfamiliar weather
> and no music at all not even the pigeons
> your ashes in frozen ground
> no comfort even in
> my rushing out at night for months afterward
> to pray for you....

Three poems by Czeslaw Milosz are translated by Joanna Warwick. Robert Crosson contributes a section of his on-going DAYBOOK. These prose poems skip through many of Crosson's preoccupations: his carpentry, his preferences for curves rather than straight lines, remembered friends, memories of being broke in Europe: "Let's not drag History into this," he wryly observes, and adds: "Writing about one's privacy makes you whore to a sense of humor." He's fascinated by the various skins we assume: "new clothes put on for trips to the bank and laundromat...same skin with a bow tie. The way Céline does it is to bullshit us into the mood at the moment. Start to laugh and we're sucked in."

Steven Ruhl's poems are coy. The first stanza of "Elegy Written in A Country Churchyard" reads as if it were spun out the brain of a kid stoned on good dope and fed on old cartoons, which he can't really focus on clearly (perhaps that's Ruhl's point, and I'm too dumb to get it.):

> Moo, moo, moo, says the little wren this morning
> in its glade of turnips and buttercups,
> cocka-doodle-doo says the horse

              in its meadow, munching the windfall apples
              near the exit ramp of the turnpike
              near our house, and meow meow meow
              says Mr. Duck, gliding in his puddle
              of ginger ale....

Steve Levine writes telegrams (real short, skinny poems)
that don't seem to wriggle much past easy statements.
This one may produce a snicker or two:

     BEAT IT

          imagine someone
          jumping up
          in an early
          Yeats poem
          screaming
          "Beat it, I
          think it's
          the cops!"

     A few comments on the reviews: Elaine Equi writes a
sweetheart review (or so it seems) of Paul Hoover's
SOMEBODY TALKS A LOT. Joanna Warwick flails fashionable
Jorie Graham's HYBRIDS OF PLANTS AND GHOSTS, and sees
the stengths and the awful flaws: all mindless Graham
lovers should read this. Tom Clark's review of ten
poets makes MAGAZINE required reading. He's one of the
rare critics/poets around who writes fearlessly, with
humor (sometimes damaging) and great originality. He
praises small press books by Jesse Glass and English Guy
Birchard, neither of whom will get much review-play, if
any, other than from Clark. Shortly, he launches into a
much-needed attack on a "new wave of pushy professor-
poets who've successfully revived the old plastic
Grecian-urn verse of the 1950's." These "Academic
Revivalists" appear in THE NEW YORKER, ANTAEUS, APR, and
in books published by Ecco Press and similar "right-
wing" eastern publishers (I begin to wonder whether the
West Coast North Point Press isn't yet another extension
of these publishers?). The names appear frequently in
the Associated Writing Programs bulletins. He proceeds:
"Naming names is usually a good idea at times like this.
How about Robert Pinsky, the wonderboy from Berkeley who
writes soporific night-before-Christmas poems for THE
NEW YORKER and gets called a genius for it by the likes
of Joyce Jenkins, publisher of POETRY FLASH. Or to pick
someone even more insufferable, how about Dave Smith?"
At the AWP, Smith's is a bigger name than Whitman's.
Clark gives a "Dangerous Furniture Award" to Michael
Blumenthal for DAYS WE WOULD RATHER KNOW, "a masterpiece
of slack escapist fantasy recently slapped into print...."
He launches into Jonathan Williams; praises F. A.

Nettlebeck's AMERICRUISER (his "favorite book of poetry in 1984"); praises the publishing by Illuminati, Peter Schneidre's Los Angeles press; and raves over Anne Waldman's MAKEUP ON EMPTY SPACE. There's probably no one who will like all of Clark's assessments--but they must be noticed; and while I disagree with him on particulars (he over-rates Nettlebeck and is too harsh on Williams) I loudly cheer his attacks on Pinsky et al. Unfortunately, he won't be much listened to. The Pinsky-Matthews-Dave Smith-Charles Wright-Halpern-Vendler axis is more than adequately sealed off from all but mutual praise. We'll keep after them, though; and who knows, we may prevail. Carry on, MAGAZINE! Carry on, Tom Clark!

THE MASSACHUSETTS REVIEW

Vol. XXIV: No. 3 (Autumn 1983). Editor: John Hicks. Memorial Hall, University of Massachusetts, Amherst, MA, 01002. $12 per year.

It's hard to fault a journal that's been around for twenty-four years and has maintained a competence rare among periodicals spawned in the Academy. Much of its long and distinguished life transpired under the egis of Joseph Langland, who has since retired. The current issue is a pleasant mix of writers, the best-known being Amy Clampitt, who is in a Visit to Greece period. Only John Tagliabue contributes anything that departs from the formalist narrative poem. Tagliabue has been writing for years, he's at his best with "Art Lesson," a tri-partite poem set in Grenoble. He meditates on Mozart, Watteau, the French Impressionists, and Debussy; in the midst of an insane world art whispers beauty. As Tagliabue falls asleep outdoors, after a day of visiting paintings, walking in the mountains, and meandering through Grenoble's beautiful parks, he falls asleep and hears "much unpublished music by Debussy."

Tagliabue satisfies at least three criteria sought by editors of the academic journal: 1). the casual first-person point of view; ie., Verse Myopia 2). the European setting (I've elsewhere called this the Academic Abroad Poem. Tagliabue teaches in Maine) 3). the traditional form--Tagliabue's poems, ostensibly journal notations, resemble Oriental poems. Other criteria used by Academic Editors are these: 4). wistful elegiac turns, often commemorating the American colonial frontier, or family histories: Frank Gaspar delights in remembering The Holyoke, an old water-heater that hasn't worked for years. Only when his great-uncle dies does Gaspar start the appliance. Andrew Hudgins employs tags ("the growing dark," an abandoned church "unable to mourn") in memory of his father.

5). Easy inspirations borrowed from Robert Frost, and occasionally from Yeats, Donne, and Roethke. e. e. cummings, one feels, is still too revolutionary. Bukowski and Ginsberg are out, for sure.   In good Frostian fashion, Amy Clampitt writes a new "Directive," following a road seldom travelled (it's a footpath) up a slope in Greece, to an old church built and adorned in the English style. Lucile Adler's truckers (they've been up early trucking apples and beef to market) drowse anticipating "steamy breaks and wedges of gray apple pie." True, they haven't fallen asleep after apple-picking--but the effect is similar. Richard Haven's tame expletives and intimate tone are reminiscent of Frost: "You've got / Order by god and let it stay / that way" and the parenthetical "at least that's how / they think of it."

6. An easy pursuit of the metaphysical...the poet as quasi-religionist/philosopher. The most blatant of these is yet another poem to God, Lucille Adler's "With Horror, Sir, Sincerely." She loves the gentle Frostian landscape, against which she positions herself to attract God's attention:

> I want you to know I am loyal,
> Not just to my own orchard and pine trees
> By a slate-cold pond, but to other pines
> Far away in gaunt lonely stands, or guarding
> Kerchiefs of lawn where it is already light
> And men and women, to whom I am loyal too, set out
>   for work.

She throws in moments of fashionable violence, all imagined and remote. Notorious for counting up all the hairs that fall from heads and feathers lost from birds, "Sir" guarantees himself much busy-work by arranging for a flock of geese to "cross paths" with a jet liner:

> White bloody
> Carcasses, red feathers, steel and flesh
> Falling on this valley explode my sleep still.

Catch that lit'rary positioning of that final adverb! Adler sees the event as "mindless," from the human point of view:

> Events, like geese and jet, like kinds of pride
> Collide, and good minds streak, mindless,
> To disaster. I know there has been an
> explosion, sir,
> And that various kinds of wings, like greatness,
> Fall. That is not my message.

Her "message" is easy to take: "Wrong's wrong." Her "mighty" Sir possesses an iron drive to kill. What we must do is to go finish the chores (ie., write your poems). This is, she says, to "face it."

Another ostensibly brainy but finally pallid effort is Sue Owen's "The Pull of Gravity." She relishes abstractions, raisins in the Christmas pudding. After moving through a series of cliché-ridden quatrains she concludes that she is "what the roots want" for "you" (for God? for a lover?), and for "blind worms." Philip Fried also finds himself buried, not in earth but in "the rich blue loam of heaven." Ozone "chants," and cosmic rays tickle and singe him as they whizz past "infinitesimally close." Fried desires "a reverse / funeral," and via verse he gives himself one. Alas, his final twist (he'll be dressed in dungarees and lowered from the skies via clothesline.) is made vapid by pretentious phrases; viz.,

> ...uncontrolled random
> diversion, exception, and fall-
> ency to ironclad law and as the final
> act of piety....

That's #7: Fried's prettified Latinate phraseology is reminiscent of bad Milton or Yeats.

The pretentious also figures in Rachel Hadas's Life-Keeping poem, "The Blue Snake." Here are the things she must do before she can bury the slithery creature: mulch the garden, fork over the compost heap, break off dead goldenglow stalks, prune the plum (she's real cute here), scour the refrigerator, remove dried spiders from the bathtub, roll up the terra cotta lion in a rag rug, pack the metronome in a shoe box, scrape out the chamberpot. Now, she's ready to bury the blue snake where she and her "you" agreed on. Sounds a lot like the break up of a marriage, doesn't it? The best part of the poem recounts "you" getting poison ivy from a "spotted kitten" that "burst out of the spiky / bushes beside the road / and rubbed against your arm / and nuzzled you." So trivial!

8. Academic connections--these are stressed in the biographical notes, a deadly variation, I think, on the Good Housekeeping Seal of Approval.

One poem alone seems to transcend the Academic Clichés: the super-casual tone, the reportage/narrative spun from the poet's experience; the image of Eden--Adam taming the beasts; the slangy interjections. <u>Tom Wayman</u> visits tigers at the Detroit Zoo at feeding time. The beasts are shy, and won't eat, so the keeper informs Wayman, until no "strangers" are present. We are treated to a pretty good view of the keeper's day with the tigers--the hassles the cats endure with each other, and the keeper's concern that the species not die out. Wayman realizes that he is not the only visitor left. He departs from the zoo, lingering long enough to imagine the young keeper settling the cats down for the night. The keeper, though, is not yet finished--he has miles to go before he sleeps: "But he has / the other parts of his work here to finish before / he feeds the birds and he goes." I feel let down.

In conclusion, I will say that I might have taken any number of other university/college journals and come to the conclusions I do here. THE MASSACHUSETTS REVIEW is merely representative of its class.

<u>NEW LETTERS</u>

Vol. 50: Nos. 2 & 3 (Winter/Spring 1984). Editor: David Ray. Judy Ray. University of Missouri--Kansas City, 5100 Rockhill Road, Kansas City, MO 64110. Quarterly. $15 per year.

This amazing compendium runs to 290 pages, and includes fiction, essays, and 120 poems. There is also a companion volume (NEW LETTERS: READER I: AN ANTHOLOGY OF CONTEMPORARY WRITING) of a like size. Under the indefatigable egis of <u>David Ray</u>, who founded the magazine in 1971, poets are well-served. Books by writers featured in NEW LETTERS have appeared, and there is a very successful National Public Radio Series, "New Letters on the Air."

In "Editorial," Ray underscores the non-elitist nature of his efforts--"We value readers and listeners alike," he writes, "as well as the poets, musicians, fiction writers, photographers and graphic artists who provide work worthy of attention. As one might expect, the poems admired by the editor have immediacy--there are seldom any cerebral high-jinks, experimental forms, or allusions to cultural arcana. That <u>William Stafford</u> opens this volume is significant--the bucolic, considered experience, often gently ironic yet affectionate, sets the tone. While there is some sexuality, it is never kinky or outrageous. There is no luxuriating in violence, although there are accidents recalled from childhood (childhood is a primary theme). Some attention to the environment--protests against our despoilations appear. And there is an ethnic mix rare in contemporary literary magazines, and an openness to older poets. Ray was the first to print the work of that national treasure, the <u>Charles Ives</u> of American poetry, <u>Alfred Starr Hamilton</u>. And his recent focusing on Indian Poetry (one entire issue was devoted to work from the massive sub-continent) is another of his single-handed efforts to inform American readers. Ray is his own editor always--and is open to all poets whether known or not--the poem first of all matters. While he does publish writers who are the darlings of Port Townsend, Squaw Valley, Breadloaf, and The Ecco Press, they never overbalance an issue. He does seem to prefer short poems--rarely do any here run over one page.   Each issue is lavish with excellent photographs and graphics.

To comment on all the poets and poems represented, is impossible. I propose to isolate some of the recurring themes and attempt to provide some sense of the variety and the quality within each theme.

POEMS OF PARENTS AND CHILDHOOD

This motif is as common here as any, and like all poems on the theme, these flirt with sentimentality. One of the best is by Isabella Gardner who wrote of childhood visits to an island off the New England Coast. With her brother George sleeping in the same room, she fantasized an entire coastal village where all the houses are lighted by whale oil lamps, and where welcoming villagers wait at their doors to bestow cookies and love. This is one of Gardner's best. For Linda Pastan, a recollected childhood is a means of confronting her own aging. Her life has had its disappointments; she took what she wanted either "too early or too late." She thinks now of "the old ladies of Cambridge," on their bicycles, with their bookbags, who "laugh through faded teeth and beckon." Failure, to them, "is just another rough cobblestone"--the message? They say that riding a bicycle and loving are alike--you never forget how. I hope to see Pastan someday riding her bike around Cambridge.

In "Alice Braxton Johnson," Michael S. Harper, recollects a childhood tragedy, when Johnson's son, Barrett drove eight-year-old Harper home, and on his return was forced off the road by bullying roughs (whites, I assume) and smashed into a tree. The old mother is crippled now, in an infirmary:

> I watch his black sole plant
> his size twelve foot jamming
> the gas, my eight-year-old hands
> at his wheel, his fight with my mother
> in mortgages, my mother's weight
> on the seasoned floor of the moon,
> the moon bleeding onto linoleum,
> my father's face in the transom
> where I was born, your house
> torpedoed on my tearless walk to school,
> and this empty chair.

Not all of these poems work as well as Harper's. Stephen Dunning mars his by spinning clichés of boyhood--ice-skating, eating cucumbers, playing in a junked car. And he throws in a couple of crows in the final lines. Vassar Miller thinks back to sloshing feet, his sister's and his, in an old wash tub, and winds off with some easy thoughts on hope.

THE JOURNAL POEM

By the "Journal Poem" I refer, quite simply, to poems that read as if they were jottings in a poet's journal of the day's events, or facts in the life of someone else that they think might interest us. These entries are then set up in verse lines and stanzas and published. Sometimes these work, more often they don't.

Martha Dickey's "Studies From Life" is 12-liner about the American painter Arthur Dove: among the few details of his life Dickey reports are these: Dove left his family "for the woman he loved" and lived with her in a boat:

> In winter when the storms got bad
> they went inland to paint
> the idea of storms.

Josephine Jacobsen fills us in on the stories she's writing:

> Working on two stories, I leave them
> arrested this morning.
> Let them take over...

She leads away from the dullness of reportage to some inventive moments.

The best of the Journal Poems is Geof Hewitt's "Missing Now 5 Days." A Vermont neighbor has disappeared. From his place a mile away, Hewitt can see her horses and mobile home. "Local rumor" so frightens Hewitt he fears to join the search. As the poem closes, Hewitt stands gazing down at her farm, thinking he sees her, or her husband, or "some other human form," possibly a murderer.

POEMS OF LOVE AND MARRIAGE

Peter Everwine masterfully contrasts a wife and her two husbands--one senses that he Everwine may possibly have been the first one. #1 responded to her dominations with off-the-wall remarks. When she'd bang the pot in the kitchen, and say "The cracked dish," he'd remark: "The princess is dancing in the ballroom." She doesn't put up with that stuff long. Husband #2, far less independent, agrees with everything. When she says "cracked dish" to him, he says, "Just as I've always thought." This second match, though secure, is boring: "The man died looking out the window. The woman died with her eyes tightly closed. Their children gave them a grand funeral and took a different name."

Toby Olson commemorates the strange girl he took out when he was fifteen: "She had more / craters in her face than I had that year." He "loved / the ancient / moon-scape of her face." In the back seat of the car kissed the "unblemished/liver of her soft lips."

Roger Pfingston develops an effective conceit for the intensity of his love for his "dear one":

I'm going to love your bones,
I mean love your bones so they will know
that they've been loved, so your flesh
will simmer with jealousy, melt and merge
with your bones, be one with your bones
and know how cold your bones have been
without love....

Marya Mannes almost crosses the line of good taste and reticence observed by most NEW LETTERS poets. Her formal sonnet celebrates the "sexual thrall" of a good fuck, despite the loneliess inherent in it. Here is the poem:

Rocking and rolling locked on tumbled bed,
priapic penis plunged in vaginal deep,
withdrawn and plunged again as exultant head
looms over face of woman whose fingers keep
pressing on urgent buttocks or sweating nape,
here is the playful, lustful, prideful male
in favorite exercise and fittest shape,
wanting no more from woman than her tail.
Wanting no more? Who knows? She wants his own,
wisely, not waiting for any tender word
other than genital. Each is alone
except when the lust they share is undeterred
by consideration of love. The moment is all,
and the blind anonymity of sexual thrall.

POLITICAL AND ECOLOGY POEMS

Robert Willson's "Putsch-1923" revisits Munich and the Nazis, creating a simply-written and powerful poem. The beer-soused Bavarians

Bitten by a lust to hate...
Swell in the streets to find
Brown shirts, bludgeons, boots.

Greg Kuzma celebrates cattails, and the joyous intimacies with nature they symbolize. The details are fresh (the plant is "a sausage / packed with seeds"), and the implication is that those days are gone, not only because we have grown up, but because so much pristine land has been despoiled. David Kherdian's short, tight "Root River" says that nature is the "home" we can never leave, where our truest dreaming occurs. Gerald McCarthy focuses on an old factory worker who turned to raising pigeons once the factory closed (the union strike failed, management closing the plant in retaliation). The old man sent notes via pigeons everywhere; none was ever answered. Yet, he was doing his own thing--self-reliant, indifferent to the "practical" world. In a smudged, polluted environment, McCarthy suggests, the best we can do is follow whatever independent drives we have. Derek Walcott writes a devastating poem on political and social changes in modern Africa, when a tribal culture has adopted Western Ways, and are imitations, and poor ones, of democracies.

HUMOROUS POEMS

There are many of these. One of the most outrageous is William Dickey's "Chickens in San Francisco." If he kept chickens, he tells us, this is how he would do it:

Deduct the cat and the dog, which are imaginary,
and you have two chickens, a male chicken and a
    female chicken
(chicken sexing is high paid work, but you have
    to travel).
They are walking around the deck. They are
    Plymouth Rocks.
The male chicken wears a buckled hat and carries
    a shotgun
and the female chicken has the New England ABC:
A is for Abstinence, B is for Boils, C is for
    Colonel Sanders.
The chickens look terribly sparse on the
    windy deck,
as if born plucked. They look at each other,
conscious of a hidden camera. They approach
    a cabbage
and under it they discover Shirley Temple.
They register the salvation of the race.
Shirley clucks a little, she is well into
what they call the skin of the part....

By contrast, Willis Barnstone's "God" seems too much of a good idea...God talks to us about the death of God. Continuing the religious motif, E. L. Mayo is far more imaginative. John Logan is wistful in his account of sitting with one of his sons on a beach near Sausalito, California. The gentle humor works. Jan Gauger's two-liner "Nothing to Remember You By" may not be worth more than a single read, but it is funny and sardonic: "You'll be leaving. The days ahead / are edged with light."

THE OLD OBJECT POEM

These poems are steeped in nostalgia, frequently deriving from a poet's youth or childhood. David Perkins considers a 1946 nickel, envying all the fingers that have oiled it, "all the change you have / made right, / all the cool black purses you have / dropped into..." The most elaborate of these poems is by Pati Hill. She actually does photocopy close-ups of portions of the old garments she writes of., viz., riding pants c. 1940 or 50. E. L. Mayo returns in memory to "a beautiful room" filled with bright rungs and gleaming furniture, a boyhood home, we assume. Etheridge Knight observes a dog urinating on a tombstone that reads "Hoosier Poet." Is it James Whitcomb Riley's? J. J. Maloney returns to the scene of a Parole Board meeting. The old door he enters is both artifact and the beginning of a nightmare:

> The oaken door through which I'll pass
> Would somehow be much better made
> If made of glass.
> The outer man I am must tread
> Into the Parole Board's dread
> Cabalistic conclave of those
>   with God's authority.

As he leaves the room, unsure of his parole, he turns for "a final look" and sees his "fate" propped in an empty wooden chair.

*   *   *   *   *

Another critic, I am sure, could easily find other themes running through this huge feast. There is enough quality so that one easily overlooks the fillers. The latter are largely by poets with big names.

<u>THE</u> <u>PARIS</u> <u>REVIEW</u>

Vol. 26: No. 91 (Spring 1984). Editors: George A.
Plimpton, Peter Matthiessen, Donald Hall, Robert B.
Silvers, Blair Fuller, Maxine Groffsky. Poetry Editor:
Jonathan Galassi. 45-39 171 Place, Flushing, NY 11358.
Poetry manuscripts to Jonathan Galassi, % The Paris
Review, 541 E. 72nd St., New York, NY 10021. $16 for
four issues.

     Since its founding some twenty-six years ago, by
Sadruddin Aga Khan, THE PARIS REVIEW has flourished as a
Palace of Art quite unto itself. So far as I know, it
appears on time (quarterly), has no financial problems,
is one of the best addresses for a. poet to have, and
pays anywhere from $15 to $100 per poem, depending on
length (according to the latest INTERNATIONAL DIRECTORY
OF LITTLE MAGAZINES & SMALL PRESSES. Its gigantic
roster of Contributing and Advisory editors, its tie-in
with the conservative Writers' Conference at Squaw
Valley, and the prose of editor Plimpton himself, all
suggest a comfortable self-assurance (smugness?)
throughout these two hundred plus pages. The presence
as Poetry Editor of Jonathan Galassi, poetry editor at
Random House also, and editor of THE RANDOM REVIEW, an
assembling of what purports to be the best poetry and
prose appearing in literary journals for a given year,
bespeaks an asafetida.

     I am happy to say that within very conservative
limits, the poetry here is better than I expected. The
featured poets write for readers with brains steeped in
Literary Culture. Alfred Corn's set of fourteen poems,
each of fifteen lines), from a book-length work in
progress NOTES FORM A CHILD OF PARADISE, is an amazing
homage to an almost throughly neglected Victorian
writer, George Meredith. Meredith's magnificent
sequence of fifty, sixteen-line sonnets, MODERN LOVE,
published in 1862, with much sardonic wit, self-probing,
and a fresh conversational tone, anatomized the
sufferings of a man and wife on the rocks. This subject
was almost non-existent before Meredith, and only D.
Snodgrass in HEART'S NEEDLE has written of it since.

In sonnet #15, Meredith enters a bedroom where his wife is either playing possum or is sleeping--Meredith is not quite sure. He is anxious to confront her with a letter he has intercepted, one she wrote to a lover, incorporating love-language she has hitherto used only for her husband. Briefly, in his Othello-jealousy/rage, he considers choking her, but instead ironically and sarcastically declares: "Sleep on: it is your husband, not your foe." The matter and tone were utterly daring in their day; the elegant diction and Shakespearean turns were not:

> I think she sleeps: it must be sleep, when low
> Hangs that abandoned arm toward the floor;
> The face turned with it. Now make fast the door.
> Sleep on: it is your husband, not your foe.
> The Poet's black stage-lion of wronged love
> Frights not our modern dames--well if he did!
> Now will I pour new light upon that lid,
> Full-sloping like the breasts beneath. "Sweet dove,
> Your sleep is pure. Nay, pardon: I disturb.
> I do not? good!" Her waking infant-stare
> Grows woman to the burden my hands bear:
> Her own handwriting to me when no curb
> was left on Passion's tongue. She trembles through;
> A woman's tremble--the whole instrument--
> I show another letter lately sent.
> The words are very like: the name is new.

Corn's narrative (I assume it's autobiographical) is of student lovers gone awry--"children of paradise." Alfred is a poet, Ann's a literature major. As a "linesmith" obsessed with verse, Al allows the "animal magnetism" between himself and Ann to fade. She continues to spend "homey evenings" transcribing her class notes or "reading that week's lesser known/Classic." She joins an evening student discussion group...the ubiquitous wine and cheese. They actually discuss MODERN LOVE, "Meredith's obsessive / Jamesian antiromance." In fact, while she's at home, absorbed reading Meredith, Alfred walks over, touches her shoulder, and waits

> ...ten counts until you lift a face
> Still vaguely fogged over with the trance of
> reading.
> "Hm?" you ask; and eyes answer full voice.

Ann moves to "a studio closer to school." Al lives now in the East Village (it's the time of "the new /Mystic-drug-and-social revolution.") Like Meredith's couple, Al and Ann are super-civilized, and promise they'll take the subway to visit each other. Al rushes to finsh his course obligations by scribbling a hasty paper on Baudelaire and Gautier. He cares mostly now about dope, "varieties of mystic thought," "perception," and "proliferating symmetries." He's psychedelic all the way. Ginsberg and Orlovsky liven him up by appearing in the neighborhood:

> Paradise Alley based in its having once
> Come up for mention in Howl. What's more the guru
> Himself an ponytailed sidekick were often
> To be seen shopping at the corner bodega.

Eventually, Alfred runs downtown to see Ann: Sergeant Pepper is big now--the psychedelic Salvation Army jackets, "blood red hyacinths / Spelling out the name that launched ten million / Discs...." (Catch those nice echoes of Chris Marlowe). She's wearing a faded shirt and bluejeans: "You are all you ever have been, ever," he exclaims. Like Meredith's hero attempting a reconciliation, his chain on silence clanks.

In March 1967 our couple attend a Be-In in Central Park: "a rainbow wave" of people dashes across the field. Alfred and Ann find their love restored:

> We stroll among much smiling innocence;
> Wonder, and doubt. The nature of a trance is
> To lift and leave a lucid calm in its wake.
> Which finds us turning to go, your hand in mine.

Perhaps some ambitious, informed critic will examine the uncannily exact reflections of Meredith's tone, style, phraseology, and metrics that scintillate throughout Corn's poem. On the surface, it might appear that Corn writes a tour de force--the opposite is true: his poem is utterly his own, its subject matter personal and contemporary. Yet he lovingly and intelligently reflects his origins. How pleased Meredith would be! Most 20th century poets, aficionados of earlier poets, generally content themselves with incorporating tags from older poets into their own poems: seldom has a poet worked so from the marrow outwards, as Corn does.

Also rife with Literary Connections is Andrew Motion's "A Lyrical Ballad," an exercise in sprung pentameter quatrains, in the bucolic mode. The occasion is a break-up with a wife. To recover, Motion is invited to Canada by "black sheep" relations. Since he's not much for riding horses, the relatives obligingly leave him to "wander alone" amidst the daffodils and lonely clouds of his own imagining. His morning routine is to walk past the village and on into a pine forest. On one excursion, he meets the equivalent of Wordsworth's old leech-gatherer (this is my parallel, not Motion's), a hippy in tartan shirt, with tangled hair, who takes him up to a minor Ararat and shows him an abandoned ark. Like figures in Wordsworth who turn up, change your life, and then disappear, this one too "vanished, politely, running his hand in silence/over the salty prow." Motion experiences no hosannahs though, and remembers this odd day to tell his estranged lover when they meet, who is, he knows, "too far away to care." This is a glossy poem--it sounds the way a good academic poem should. Motion is too self-obsessed to give either nature or the Canadian relatives a fair shake.

Amy Clampitt travels to Grasmere in the English Lake District and, for some 150 lines, inhabits Dorothy Wordsworth's psyche. The subject is Dorothy's incestuous attraction for her brother William, even after his marriage, and the mix of winsome unawareness her famous journals reveal. Clampitt incorporates passages from the journal into her own poem, and, in the portions that are hers, does a nice anachronistic jig, nicely imitating Dorothy's prose. One of my own early books, CONNECTIONS: IN THE LAKE DISTRICT (Anvil Press, London, 1972), covered much of this same territory, also using the collage technique and Dorothy's Journals. I appreciate Clampitt's skill. When she writes in her own voice, she still manages to evoke Dorothy's. This erotic passage is a good example:

>   ...birds singing; the sacred stain
> of bluebells on the hillsides; fiddleheads
> uncoiling in the brakes, inside each coil
> a spine of bronze, pristinely hoary;
> male, clean-limbed ash trees whiskered
> with a foam of pollen; bridelike
> above White Moss Common, a lone wild cherry
> candle-mirrored in the pewter of the lake.

Jordan Smith's "Lucky Seven," is also in a nineteenth century mode. His smooth, informal iambic hexamters resemble those Arthur Hugh Clough fashioned for his casual-toned, limpid epic, The Bothie of Tober-na-Vuolich(1848), yet another unjustly neglected Victorian masterpiece. Smith is on a retreat for study and recuperation, much as Clough's undergraduates were on a study vacation in Wales. Smith's poem, which runs to some 300 lines, is set in Saratoga Springs, New York. His themes are: Saratoga in its early turn-of-the-century heyday; Smith as a child on a family excursions to the mountains; and Smith's future. He works his way through a storm-strewn landscape, coming at last to a lake (One of the best moments in Clough's poem is an over-view of a tarn.)   Here is Smith:

And a weasel sprang out, reddish, swollen,

> spitting with rage
> That lashed his limbs like a sudden wind. Shaken,
>   I slipped, rolled
> Down along bare rock that led nowhere but to a cliff's
>   edge.
> Below me was the calm sheen of a mountain lake at
>   noon--
> Bright glare on the horizon, and the stones
>   and branching snags
> Clear in the shallow bay, my path's snarled,
>   downfallen pattern
> Distanced, altered by the tannic stain of the
>   lake water
> Into the reflective silence of a daguerrotype.

Hayden Carruth takes his opening cue from John Milton's sonnet on his blindness, and, with Schopenhauer's blessing, develops a wonderful satire of "children of the middle class" who, like their parents, are "never things-in-themselves." In this devastating conclusion, Carruth almost gleefully depicts his isolation and his loathing:

> The spirea dies, the
> little nebulae of viburnum wink out in
>   willing
> whatness, but the children's shrieks of bliss
>   and triumph
> are merciless, raging from another world, another
>   time,
> in casualties I cannot properly discern or
>   identify,
> so that all understanding is blocked and thrust
>   back
> as mere knowledge, odious data, nauseating
>   demonstrations,
> these relentless present children of the middle
>   class.

In Lavina Blossom's "After the Harlequin" there's a tale of an overly-protected woman's excursions into love. She runs away from her father, turns tough and outspoken ("false bravado"), links up with a handsome man whose advances she rejects. Then, in a plot worthy of Barbara Cartland, she marries a dude she thinks is penniless, but finds, in fact, that he is one of the continent's richest men. "And here our story begins..."

A pair of poems, one by Michael Benedict, the other by Tom Disch, treat matters dear to poets. The former digs at pretentious intellectualizing and probes "Economic Reality" and "Love" as appropriate topics for verse. In a Capitalist World, love alas, matters less than economics. Although poetry counts for naught, Love has a way of "popping up obnoxiously, or perhaps/cheerfully, right in the middle of everything." Disch is damned clever, satirizing poets enamored of grants, fellowships, and prizes: "True mediocrity," he tellingly observes, like genius, "aggregates into nodes." Gather a dozen medocrities, these nodes together, and you "have a department":

        The only <u>genuine</u> innovation
In the arts has been the belated recognition accorded
        mediocrity
By forming poets into Schools and Offices of Poetry,
By helping them most generously to help themselves,
By encouraging their application to all forms of
        application blank...

I can't imagine a single poet who won't love this, for Disch is so elusive that nary a poet, no matter how stuffed gormandizing at the grants and awards troughs, will think Disch has him in mind. I wish he had named names!

These then are my conclusions about THE PARIS REVIEW: if you wish to write for it, be sure your brains show, be familiar with some old styles and modes, refer to the great authors you have read, and have a bent for the casual and the satiric. Further, don't hesitate to write longish poems--PR likes them. My guess is, though, that because of the mag's reputation, hundreds of poets submit work. Be warned: this is one poet's experience--over seven months ago I sent Galassi a chunk of a long work in progress I thought might interest him. I have yet to hear...although I did enclose a SAE with sufficient postage. With all those editors on the masthead, it's hard to know which one will listen, if indeed any one will.

<u>PERMAFROST</u>

Vol. 5: No. 2(Spring 1983). Editors: Roberta Roth
Laulicht and David Sims. English Department, University
of Alaska, Fairbanks, AL 99701. Twice yearly. $5 p.a.

When PERMAFROST arrived I was sure it would be
representative of a number of regional lit mags, with
the strengths and weaknesses that implies. I was wrong:
this generous mix of poetry and fiction is only
tangentially Arctic--while Western poets dominate (the
editors seem fond of poets from the American Southwest),
there are Easterners.

In a "Note," the editors comment on the manuscripts
they've received--there's a preponderance of "disturbing
themes," centered on contemporary America--"a world so
full of inapplicable sexual and social conventions, a
world changing so rapidly in its values and priorities,
that a person must constantly be questioning his or her
place in it." The editors found "repeated instances of
alienation, sexuality, and violence." They apologize
(and it's regrettable they feel they must do this) to
readers who might be "disturbed by some of the explicit
scenes."

<u>Jack Heflin</u> opens with a pair of innovative poems.
"Dear Reader, With Apologies" is layered with violence.
Our cage waits; "knots of horror" in his eyes subdue us,
and he carries us to a turret to view the stars. The
second piece is in a Latino voice, one that regales us
with scraps of a life, a family, and his obsessions. The
speaker withdraws from the modern world; he sits
"forever chattering of corn and kings." Here is a
representative stanza:

> Notice that oil pooling around the mound,
> rich and black like a bowl of turtle beans,
> the authorities have not seen it.
> Only you have seen it....

<u>Al Schultz</u> re-evokes the isolation he felt in the early
'sixties, in an attic room in Portland, Oregon--one
man's life as he waits on the threshold of adulthood,
gazing out through his single window at the city below:
"...all the sparkly little rows of the world / spread
below like what one might see, // spinning over, of a
gentle, new planet." One might fuss over the funny
syntax here--but a poignancy emerges, of late-adolescent
loneliness keenly remembered, those "high school
midnights"

                     --without wife
          or mother or child, without color

       or pain. Thus I rode in my frail
       wooden mountain that stood and rattled
       its one gabled window for all the black wind.

    Judith Skillman's "Insomnia" seems "written" rather
then felt. The opening line clues us in to a workshop
poem full of recipe-images--it sounds the way a good
poem should: "The night is hung with phosphorous/and
lit bridges./ Every street is a memory." And this is
messy: toes, ankles, knees, and arms "ache for milk."
Cleopatra's bath? Our fingers, palms, and forearms tell
us, she says, that "we must swing the right circles." I
fear that's what she does with this entirely safe and
boring poem, ie., wing the right circles.

    Ken Prichard is one of the best poets here. His
"Doppelgonger" (sic) is fresh, imaginative, scary. It's
a love poem for his double, a threatening extension of
himself, a glue-sniffer, stalker of cats roaming golf-
courses, an Indian prowling the neighbor's yard. When
the Double fades, Prichard is left listening to
whispering spiders and watching slugs guzzle beer. It's
afternoon, a dull time for most of us--but not for
Prichard: this is what his double tells him:

       it is time to slit
       our tongues on blackberry briars,
       and mix our adrenaline with a kiss.

How does Prichard respond?

       My blood is algae
       when you come with the smell
       of dead turtles wiped across your chest.
       It lays you down in the moss
       among ferns and monkey vines
       that swing you over creeks
       swollen with carp.

I wish the poem had ended here: but Prichard can't
resist setting a final fancy plug that we are all
compost (thanks Walt Whitman). "Our mother" carries "old
bread...wrapped in corncloth" out to the compost pile.
Despite my fussing, this is an effective poem, and
Prichard is a poet to watch.

    Two settings of Franz Kafka's letters to Felice
Bauer, "transcribed" by Carol V. Davis are not good:
here is a clumsy moment from the first one:

       In the
       contained

             train car,
             a hallucination
             accompanies me...

Franz must be squirming in his grave. The second is
better, and concludes with an image of F. diving into
Felice's photograph, surfacing with her in his arms.
Nicholas Rinaldi starts off a poem for Jennifer
boringly. He's sitting at restaurant in Venice hoping
she'll show up. The narcissism of the first twenty
lines is a real turn-off--like all good narcissist-
poets, Rinaldi thinks he's the cynosure of all waiters,
customers, and passing priests. He loses me when he
trips into the mind of a passing old woman carrying her
crocheted bag of fruits and veggies. Since she does not
"notice" him, he notices her: and he sentimentally
reports that she is thinking of a clock hanging in her
mountain girl-hood home..."a clock with feeling." He
knows that "she is not Jennifer." One would hope not.
There are still about twenty lines to go (it's a long
poem), and I am glad I persisted. The closing half is
effective, as he fights his hunger for Jennifer.

    Jon Davis's "The Young Wife" excites me. The
lengthy lines are flawless, the motif of the poem--the
wife's sense of her estrangement from her young husband
is moving. She waits in bed.   In Nature, birds are
grossly plump and sated:

        ...plump grosbeaks
     lurch like rodents in the cottonwoods, a robin--
     puffed up, violent--perched stiff as a thumb.

Wonderful! The "man" is frightening: he comes through
the gate, "wild-eyed" and grunting. "His mouth grows
slack, like an infant's." Once in the house, he watches
endless TV. The wife feels betrayed by a world which had
promised her more. The house (the fresh marriage) has
gone awry: "Our yard grows wild. I don't ask him to mow
or trim. / I don't look him in the eye." At dinner
he's boring, talks only of his work and the plumbing.
Afterwards, he leaves the house, staying out until dawn.
The wife waits and waits:

     listening to the wisteria--grown thick
     as a man's arm--as it grappled with shingles,
     twisting and creaking, thatching the windows
        and doors.

    The first Alaskan poem is Mary Lou Sanelli's "A
Change of Season," written from the point of view of a
young Indian bride caught cross-culturally between Cable
TV, REDBOOK, and her Indian heritage. She's not the
sanitized middle-class honky bride--guests throw puffed

wheat instead of Uncle Ben's rice, and she wears long underwear and forgets to shave her legs:

       All the hoopla. White gown and fancy cake.
       New to young girls on your island where
       Customs change with Cable TV and Redbook
       Delivered in stacks from the floatplanes
       With pretty brides wearing pretty smiles of
       Perfect teeth on the covers but for her,
       Your grandmother, things were different.
       She sat in the bow of a canoe for hours
       Waiting for the herring run with a net and
       The cold wrapped her shoulders like a wool
              shawl
       Only thicker..

Sanelli's maiden loses her virginity in a car--and not without some humor: her head "hit the steering wheel and the horn / Went off as he entered with a blast." The grandmother's experience, again, was different: when she was fifteen she was taken from home to another clan, made ready with beads and feathers, and taken to the "first night."

       when, side-by-side, she the Eagle would be
    Taken by the young Raven next to the firelight in a
    Longhouse with everyone listening.

Rachel Nova, a Seattle poet contributes two lyrics nicely fashioned around Arctic imagery. Both are love poems. In the first, the affair seems over:

                 Wind curls
       the tundra; the frosted hummocks
       crackle. Over icefalls, the sandhill cranes
       spiral, span the crevasses ranging winter.

In the second, she has left the lover's cabin, imagines the ice charring the window, observes the lover reading a book and drinking whiskey, and wonders if he sees her coat in his closet, her boots at the door, when he steps outside to "chart the rise of constellations/and the falling stars." I believe in these poems: there's no nonsense, ie., pretentious writing.

       David Chorlton seems to struggle over a poem not too dissimilar from Wordsworth's "Michael," although Chorlton is a tad more primitive. A smelly shepherd's son goes off to the city. Workshop images spoil the cloth: an example--young women (the old women are busy shrinking "to fit their embroidery") "punish" the still hard ground "to open its pores." The girls bind their hair "in flowered cotton / as they press against the wet heart of the fields." Betty Lowry also doesn't have her poem well in hand--she writes pretentiously of what old Chinese poets meant: "In Ming and Ch'ing the muse / redundant said of poetry / that it would rise again / as sure as paper boats dissolved / along the banks of the Tsinghai." _Redundant_ says it, alas. _Clifford Saunders_ rather mindlessly splashes rhymes: _moon, spoon, wound, saloon, loon, pantaloons, dunes_. He's another denizen of the U. of Arizona MFA program.

PERMAFROST is pretty good. A handful of poems are as exciting as any I've read over the past few weeks. And it is not at all an hermetically regional journal. Refreshing also is its emphasis on young talents. Unlike lesser mags seeking audiences, they don't parade inferior poems by celebrity poets.   PERMAFROST is in its sixth year--may it flourish!

THE POETRY REVIEW: A MAGAZINE OF POETRY, TRANSLATIONS OF POETRY, AND ESSAYS PUBLISHED SEMI-ANNUALLY BY THE POETRY SOCIETY OF AMERICA

Vol. 1: No. 2 (1983). Editor: F. D. Reeve. Advisory Board: Philip Appleman, Hayden Carruth, Siv Cedering, Pamela Hadas, Donald Junkins, Gardner McFall. Subscription with membership in the Poetry Society of America.

One result of the recent blood-baths waged by the old guard factions of the Poetry Society of America with younger, more progressive voices (The old guard lost.) is the appearance of THE POETRY REVIEW. I had hoped that the REVIEW (this issue runs to 110 pages) would reflect the changed climate better than it does. The language is safe and sanitized--the old poetesses with three names who long dominated the Society (in company with Dr. Alfred Dorn, et. al.) will find little to disturb them.

A scrutiny of a number of opening lines reveals the tone. First, there are an overwhelming number of tepid first-person starts, of so little distinction most seem interchangeable one with another. These examples are each from different poems. The authors shall remain nameless:

I don't know the names of things...

I am too weak to leave the infirmary...

ah my words...

And when it was time / I came to the
          Petrified Forest...

Filter me like rain/nucleus to nebula,
          forever...

I've not written an Aswan Dam poem.

Whenever I bring her flowers she cries.

The year I traced over pictures / in
          PARADISE LOST...

My father threw me off the deep end...

And so I capture / the sun on that bridge
          the cows...

<u>I</u> <u>am</u> <u>the</u> <u>old</u> <u>lady</u>....

A few poems appear to depart from this tedious norm, but, alas, once you work through you find that most reflect trivial moments in the poet's life. Two of the best are in homage to <u>John Berryman</u>. <u>Christina Starobin</u> writes effective imitations of Berryman. So good are they, in fact, that one forgives her descent into the dreary solipsism at the end. Yet, Berryman pointed the way. THE DREAM SONGS are among the most blatantly ego-centered poems ever written. <u>Ruth Feldman</u> also gives the college try, writing of old trees that "do not give up without a struggle" and of a painting by <u>Carvaggio</u> of Peter and a tavern maid, as Peter is about to hear that rooster crow. Feldman, alas, is not up to the occasion, and writes cadenced lines that bounce along like a rocking horse with a missing wheel. And some of her enjambments are unfortunate. At least she deserves credit for eschewing the ego-poem.

<u>Constance Urdang</u> writes impressively within the mode of the conventionally ornate poem crammed with literary adjectives and phrases. She is something of a <u>Gustave Moreau</u> of poetry. Here is the ending of a poem to a girl who was called "Lizard":

My lively, my lovely, my jewel-eyed,
Cloisonné-mailed, cloth of gold,
Field of a thousand flowers,
Lizard, you have illuminated.

Urdang is adept, though, at both the ornate and the simple styles. In "A Little Elegy" she mixes the two. What could be simpler than this passage?

She was one with the mothers
Whose children have disappeared. She was
        one with those
Who come carrying in a single bundle
All they have in the world...

The poem concludes with some unfortunate posturing in the Ornate Style:

Let rain be her requiem.
The steady unemphatic drizzle
That drenched the mourners on the pale
        hillside
Where they lowered her ashes into the
        sodden earth:
The monotone of the dull rains of December.

The passage seems unfelt, enervated. The first line with its easy alliteration warns us of a flagging

inspiration. And the phrases ("unemphatic drizzle,"
"pale hillside," "sodden earth") are flatulent. And
later, when she avers that "soft summer showers" in an
abandoned garden beyond "weeping windows" are sighing
the night away, she employs the tired pathetic fallacy
with a vengeance.

George Keithley, with "Wild Flowers," writes a
moving elegy to his mother. He is unabashedly personal:
"I remember my mother at some moment / of every daylight
hour." "Never will I leave her." He used to pick wild
daisies and bluebells for her--she'd cry.   Years later,
he picks more flowers, thinking she is alive, and is
overwhelmed by thundering horses--literal, yes, but also
images for his own grief and lost childhood. These
horses are "huge" and "unbridled"

                         black as trees
    when a storm shakes its wet hair
    over their limbs. Routed by the rain,
    I run through the trembling grass--
    I cry out, I cry out for my mother.

Another fine poem, also in the conservative
tradition, is Edwin Honig's six-part "Remembering
Hornets." Honig employs the first-person, drops in the
occasional lovely-sounding phrase ("the legendary
lastingness," "the momentous morning," "sullen memory,"
etc.), and writes of love. What makes his suite
memorable is that he transcends the frayed modes. He's
passionate over his love-failures, the accidental death
of a younger brother, and moon-walks. Despite the
vastness of space and time, we are limited on earth to
our successes and failures to love.   Here are Honig's
closing lines. He recalls sleeping men and women whose
dreams are visited by painful ghosts, "lumps of sullen
memory / like corpses the rippling / flood heaves up."
Also, in sleep,

        long-absent bodies
    ...reach for one another
    with endearments pulsing wordless
    as hornets in the rain....

Then, one recalls

        the sudden lull
    of couples rising and retreating
    in the tides. Were they alerting
    one another how to die?

    Where could they have learned to open
    body unto body, recreating flesh
    yearning to liquefy

before coming residue?

After so much recalled, so many tried
and quietly subsiding in the mind,
the truth, at first touch, still burrows
like a crab blackening in mud.

That final image is a master-stroke, focusing as it does
on a crab in what seems like primal ooze. Here, and not
on the moon, nor along transcendental leaps to imagined
nirvana-paradises, Honig insists, is where we work our
destinies.

     I had hoped to write a far more positive appraisal
of THE POETRY REVIEW. Certainly, journals wishing to
maintain the status quo in writing, should, it seems to
me, showcase the very best of that writing. That's my
complaint. Perhaps the advisory board (if they do
function in selecting work), with the exception of
Carruth, are too conservative--very staid members of
Establishment publishing and Poetry Society of America
activities. It does seem that this journal should serve
a broad spectrum of poets (most American poets join the
Society to enjoy the numerous and prestigious Spring
awards). The Old Guard of the Society, losers in those
bloody internecine struggles, still seemed to prevail,
at least in this issue.

<u>PULPSMITH</u>

Vol. 3, No. 3 (Autumn '83). Editors: Harry Smith,
Sidney Bernard, Tom Tolnay, William Packard, et al. The
Generalist Association, Inc., 5 Beekman St., New York,
NY 10038. Quarterly. $2 per issue.

PULPSMITH, now in its 4th year, aims for
readability, and it succeeds. Taking its format from
the pulp mags of the 30's and 40's, it's so handsome it
entices one to keep it on the coffee table, in the john,
or by the bed, ready for casual reading, whenever the
urge strikes. There's a smorgy of stories, articles,
interviews, and poems. Since <u>William Packard</u>, formerly
of NEW YORK QUARTERLY merged his efforts with PULPSMITH,
the interview is more of a feature--including interviews
of "pioneer pulp writers," conducted, I hope, by <u>Donald
Phelps</u>, that specialist in pop culture arcana. As for
poetry, this issue seems representative of earlier
PULPSMITHs, 23 poems scattered throughout, some as
fillers, most featured beautifully on their own pages,
all printed in adobe-colored ink. Each page is lovingly
designed, often with spirited graphics with an old-
fashioned turn. Poets can't expect better.

How good are the poets? <u>May Sarton</u> and <u>Daniel
Berrigan</u> are names here. Lesser-known are <u>Hugh Fox,
Yusef Kommunyakaa</u>, <u>H. L. Van Brunt</u>, and <u>Geraldine
Little</u>. The other fourteen are relative unknowns.
Eight poems are clustered as "Modern Love Poems"; the
others are scattered.

How good are the poems? Few are badly written; and
they are a mix of formalist and free verse. A prize-
winner, <u>Raeburn Miller</u>, contributes a rather tepid
English sonnet. The prize she received is "The Edna St.
Vincent Millay Award." Perhaps the editors were looking
for a conventional piece with all the grandiose tomb-
language characteristic of <u>Millay</u>'s poems. Too bad--for
Miller writes on an up-to-date topic: "cosmic
particles" bending through "cloud chambers."

<u>May Sarton</u> employs rhymed stanzas (abcabc, with a
variation in the first stanza) to embroider the idea
that covering nasturtiums against expected frost is like
covering over a friendship: after the marriage,
cherishing and building together occur--a covering over,
I gather, against the frosts seeping in over the hills.
The best of the conventional poems is <u>Geraldine C.
Little</u>'s "St. Francis: Dying Towards Light." In
thirteen terza rima stanzas, the Saint reports on his
life, how it changed in a flash from an indulgent life

in Assisi, to asceticism, to a vision of his coming death.

There's but one coy moment in PULPSMITH verse--in Linda Potmesil's "menage." Her loafers, at night, "sleep / one over the other / like the cat's front paws." And then, as if we haven't gotten the point, she tells us that those loafers "are self-contained." And so is she, since she's just split from a lover, and seems to like it. Or is it that she's abandoning her loafers, graduating to heels?

In case the reader tires of high seriousness, there is a kinky piece, Hugh Fox's outrageous "Hitchiker's Guide to Times Square." Since Jagging off is good for one's health, Fox trips off to a "jag-off parlor," invests in five bucks worth of quarters, enters a booth, and because of the stench of piss, leaves and complains to the management. This is not his day:

> Times Square is a blowjob
> just waiting to explode,
> my prick's Ground
> Zero at Alma Gordo...
> I go into Parlor Two...

More frustration, and this life-motto: "Man does not live by / Cum alone." Fox spins along after that Universal Onanist Orgasm. I won't reveal whether or not he finds it.

David Citino supplies another sex-frustration poem: Sister Mary Appassionata details "the Resourcefulness of Demons" for her theology class. The poem is tightly written and compellingly imagined. The details ring true:

> I'm in the middle of abstinence
> and beauty strides into the room
> on taut, ample thighs, imposing
> itself between decades of the rosary....

This earthy sister finds evidence of demons in "the wrinkles and creases / of a hot night's sleep" and "by what's /left in the bathwater when / I rise steaming and clean." In a way, the poem is a crowd-pleaser--we all like reading about the human sides of saints and angels.

PULPSMITH features the abortion issue. Menke Katz writes for aborted babes who have lost their roles as future "pilots, poets, presidents, shoe-shiners, and astronauts." For the Flip side, there's a short "Message for Rev. Falwell," by Editor Harry Smith, who encourages the Rev. to follow through on his notion that "the earliest fetus" is "a tiny human" and hold funerals for them, honoring them with "the tiniest tombstones--or thimble urns." Build an "exquisite tomb of the Unknown Embryo" on the White House lawn.

In "Fidelity," Daniel Berrigan arraigns the world of insane presidents and generals. He seeks solace in a world of New York City "freaks" and "minority spirits," who've "lost again." He is one of them--as is the dying wife of the old picture framer friend, who's propped in her wheelchair "like a cauliflower." When she dies, her wheelchair, is "lodged like an embolism/in the body politic." She is a lotus seen against the backdrop of a horrid world:

On this foul foot path
mule track, death mile, oblivion alley, bloody pass
Broadway, pith and paradigm of the world, cutting the
50 states of Amnesia like a poisoned pie; a
     swollen Styx
     an Augean drain ditch

     a lotus blooms.

Two poems are elusive. Yusef Komunyakaa's "The Vindictive" is well-written--there's nary a syllable out of joint, or a false grind. Moreover, there's a jolt of passion about a third of the way down when the strange jailer opens the iron door and walks in to stare down at the prisoner he will eventually touch and kiss. Wagner's Ring of the Nibelung is playing, and there's the odor of mignonette. Beauty and disease. Pain and love. The jailer

     tightens his mystical sleephold--
     a carbuncle of joy
     underneath his kiss.

Lance Lee's "a chordal ecstasy" appears to be about an old man, an original, who early discovered "the intervals of the chords." He found "the key to play himself / the world." He's like Robert Browning's mysterious poet, talked about by the Spanish dandies in "How It Strikes a Contemporary." Lee's speaker is a poet, or artist, it appears, who took cues from the old man's reshaping of the ocean. Approaching death: ("a baited hook" seems to dangle "from another world" to catch him) leads to some pretty wild behavior on the part of the acolytes: they smash fruit in their ears, and a "black drool of seeds" runs down their cheeks. It's their turn: they teach him "silence, / how no one loves to change, / how to die is our only charge." They hollow out his head, all to no avail. For he continues to haunt them, and particularly the speaker, who must now move on to his own chordal ecstasies. The old mentor's tongue is "swollen as a loaf of bread/ with unspeakable song...that deep writhing silence from/which all song/takes flight." Lee is an impressive poet.

The love poems are a mixed bag. Geraldine Greig saps her poem by overusing fancy Shakespearean phrases: "beyond all acquaintance," "shift and pull of desire," "pathways of life," etc. Ron Houchin contributes an endearing take on a heavy woman ("she is the housekeeper / Of a bankrupt god") who eats a huge bowl of chili on her day-off:

        Her back and shoulders
Are bent, like a bear's, giving in to pleasure.
I love her. The way
She belts down life reaffirms it.

Nick Bozanic waxes sentimental over his child-daughter, and like all fathers of feeling, tries to take her futures pains as his own, by (cliché) feeling his heart chill up with winter. Franz Douskey inserts a pair of fine moments in an otherwise dull poem: he asks his woman to wear something he won't recognize: "a brown flower, or a dried monkey." Later on, he tells her that her breasts burn holes in his trench coat.

PULPSMITH is a good mix, and, according to THE INTERNATIONAL DIRECTORY OF LITTLE MAGAZINES & SMALL PRESSES, they do pay.

<u>SAMISDAT</u>

Vol. 37: #3 (1983). Editor: Merritt Clifton. Box 129.
Richford, Vt 05476. $15 for 500 pp. (Includes the
magazine, chapbooks, etc.). $25 for 1,000 pp. $150 for
all future publications.

     SAMISDAT's themes, as announced on the cover page,
are: beer, sex, running, baseball, peace, love, ecology,
freedom. Clifton is a one-man ecology Galahad, fighting
the awesome battles of acid rain (he lives not far from
the Canadian border) and environmental pollution. He is
also a literary dynamo, writing his own poetry and
fiction, and publishing lots of work by poets and
writers living not only in the wastes of upper New
England but all over the country. He has launched
important poets, among them <u>W. D. Ehrhart</u>, <u>Deborah
Knaff</u>, and <u>Cathy Czapla</u>. He is a trove of information
on alternative press journals and books, and he shares
his wisdom in his pages. He is ruthless in his
editorials and in his reviews. He also writes a regular
column for SMALL PRESS REVIEW.

     Like most of Clifton's publications, SAMISDAT is
printed by direct-image offset. Imaginative, off-the
wall artwork, like the poems, are scattered throughout
the review sections and the fiction. The look and feel
is not dissimilar from an old FARMERS' ALMANAC.   In
fact, issues look ephemeral--as soon as the seeds are
bought, the sun-charts consulted, and the seeds in,
relegate SAMISDAT to the outhouse for further savoring.
By that time, the next batch of SAMISDAT stuff will be
along to help you through the hot summer, through the
harvest, and then through winter.

     SAMISDAT is fashioned for ordinary consumption,
daily food--it's to be read right along with your oats,
or while waiting for the maple syrup to drip from the
tree, or as your brushpile burns. Nothing about this
journal smacks of poetry-lovers in academic clothing in
ivory towers: in fact, there's little writing that
requires the use of a dictionary or encyclopedia. And
there are rarely any sophisticated forms so dear to the
<u>Robert Pinskys</u>, <u>Jorie Grahams</u>, <u>William Matthewses</u>,
<u>Gerald Sterns</u>, and <u>Richard Howards</u> of the poetry world.
If it's not barn-made, forget it! In a way, these are
poems for readers who are too busy taking in the hay,
making jam, ice-fishing, or drinking beer and playing
baseball to make subtle forays into the sophisticated
poetry world.

Let's scrutinize some of these 26 poems. Robert Joe Stout has a well-crafted and gentle "Clearing Up the Garden," which suits the image of the Farmers' Almanac well. As he stacks split pumpkins beside a fence, he hears a pair of robins.

> They were in separate trees
> across the alley--winter visitors
> for whom frosty mornings and weeks of rain
> were balmy and bountiful weather
> after their flight south from the snow-streaked
>   Arctic.

Stout turns to the chore of pulling up volunteer walnut shoots (perhaps "sprouted from some forgetful squirrel's hoarding"). He imitates the robins' call, as he tugs at the walnut stems. The chore defeats him: the roots resist. He leaves the garden, notices a breeze in an oleander hedge, tips his cap.

SAMISDAT likes homespun fillers: Deborah Knaff hopes to find that "while a thousand defeats don't add up to victory, they can add up to a worthwhile life." Here's a raunchy filler, a 6-liner by Robert R. Hentz, ostensibly based an an ancient "Parsidian proverb": "The taste of an asshole/should incline to shit." Do we squirm, wondering if our own bungholes are sanitary? Do we tack Hentz' shortie on our bathroom wall? Imagine SAMISDAT as a raunchy poet-figure, clad in manure-covered farm shoes, with wood-ticks in his beard, his body pasted with poems. We can see him, on his side of the stream, giving the smelly finger to the conservative/academic poetry clones gathered across the river, beneath the beeches and pines, having their summer Poetry Confabs. The editor himself fashions one of these rowdy little-fuckers, in the form of a mail label, as a reminder that the reader's subscription has expired.

SAMISDAT

> Mark Phallus
> 2 Short
> Gaylordstown, New York
> 14746

(infinity)

SAMISDAT engages in some husband and wife foreplay. Michael Glaser riffs sardonically on the inadequacies of males confronting female sexual mysteries:

> Beside their swollen bellies, we husbands
> slouch while our women whisper sweet sounds
> like 'ooh' and 'ahhh' and 'mmm'...
>
> Though we know the music we feel
> between our legs is a dull tune
> thudding and awkward against
> the menses, the ocean and moon....
>
> Flexing muscles, we lure these women
> into dangerous worlds. We swell bellies
> and urge them to adore us, to sing
> 'oooh' and 'ahhhh' and 'mmmm'...
> to make us strong.

Clifton contributes this tough take on male-female issues: men turn what they become, or touch, to blood and violence:

OUR FIRST WOMAN PRIEST

> "If men could get pregnant,"
> she shrieked,
> "abortion would be a sacrament!"
> Like blessing the troops,
> first kill, gang-rape,
> witchburning,
> slitting a virgin's throat.

Families matter. Peter Desy reflects on himself as a child, in 1940, sitting between his parents on a couch, trying to decide which one he loves the best. He makes a painful choice, against mom:

> I say I love you both, but, Mother,
> you go stern; and, Father,
> you only smile and I know
> this is not your doing, so I reach
> for your hand and Mother stiffens
> and her mouth goes hard.

Susan Packie writes of children turned into lab specimens. They've had it rough from the start--flame-retarded pajamas, watery powdered milk low in nutrients, teddy-bears with lethal eyes and noses. Elders who test these goodies on the little tikes wonder at their lethargy, dizziness, and lack of coordination. Miriam A. Cohen's "What is Known" should give a chill to any Vermont housewife sending her kids off to the school bus:

> This rainy morning
> somewhere

children are tracing their left hands
or fingerpainting cows and trees,

objets d'art,
each signed
TO MOMMY: I LOVE YOU VERY MUCH XXX,

as the teacher glides from table to table,
smiling, complimenting, and
putting red checks in her book.

Later the pictures will be placed
on refrigerator doors
by mothers
who know they're running out of time.

Thomas Armstrong's "Anette" harrowingly details the transformation, by the public school, of a sad dyslexic girl into a zombie:

Now, thank District, she's finally cured.
She sits somewhere in a roomful of remediates,
straightened out and upright,
sunken low and lifeless,
her education complete.

Ida Cruzkatz writes the funeral poem ubiquitous to lit mags with a common touch: Iowa poets seem to love 'em. "Selma: In Memoriam" is cuts above most of the genre, and is, I think, the best poem here. In lean, subtly-broken lines, fraught with strong images, Cruzkatz is lethal in her depicition of the insensitive rabbi (Selma was "just a mother," he says), and unsparing of her mother's difficult life. For 30 years she sold franks, fries, and cokes in stadiums--this the rabbi overlooks, as he does "her joy" when she earned enough tips to buy pizza for the family. She did have lovers occasionally (her husband died young), men who "helped break / the stench of a two-room place, / with her sons in bunk beds / and her on the Castro in the parlor." In good rabbi-fashion, the rabbi directs the family away from the casket to the surviving sons in the first row. This is how the poem ends:

He buried her there in the parlor,
covered her, shrouded her,
completely disguised her
into the form of her sons.
Hers is the casket of blue vest and jacket,
replete with both black tie and cuff-links.
He will address her as Selma, Deborah, or mother;
either way,
it is the front row--
the blue,

that must be watched.

Among political and ecological poets are these:
Michael Suarez is satiric about a journalist's jaunt to
El Salvador. The dude is awake enough to know that he
can never enter any real horrors:

I left knowing that
only the calf roasting alive
can feel the fire....

Robert McLean writes of a poisoned fishing reservoir--
not even carp can live. Walt Franklin hungers for a
return to natural food--snails, rabbit, pheasant,
fish..."no mystic fruit," fresh food taken to the
marketplace "unsealed, uncovered, fresh."

SAMISDAT is easily one of a handful of the most
readable magazines around, and it shares pizzazz with a
network of young, randy publications; viz, John
Elsberg's BOGG, Richard Peabody's GARGOYLE, David
Spicer's RACCOON, Ron Androla's NORTHERN PLEASURE and
Steven Doering's RANDOM WIERDNESS. Clifton writes me,
acknowledging his direct influence on these mags: MANGO,
BUG TAR, THE PUB, QUESTER, TAURUS, FIRE, and the Adastra
Press, among other. The snooty reader may complain that
Clifton et al (Robin Michelle Clifton, who writes "The
Pillory," is, according to the grapevine, one of the
sexiest women in the small lit mag world) are as
hermetic in featuring a brand of poet they admire as are
the editors of IRONWOOD, THREE PENNY REVIEW, or IOWA
REVIEW. And this is true. Also true is the fact that
SAMISDAT sizzles and keeps you reading. And once your
crops are in and your babe is weaned, it doesn't matter
whether whether you truck your SAMISDAT publications
off to the out-house or not: what you've read will
linger inside your d. t. (viz., digestive track) and
will move you, much as an orgy of peanut-eating might on
Saturday night spent before the tube, or listening to
the Prairie Home Companion on National Public Radio.

<u>SULFUR:A LITERARY TRI-QUARTERLY OF THE WHOLE ART</u>

#10 (1984). Editor: Clayton Eshleman. Contributing
Editors: Michael Palmer, Jerome Rothenberg, Eliot
Weinberger. Correspondents: James Clifford, Marjorie
Perloff, Jed Rasula, John Yau. 852 S. Bedford St., Los
Angeles, CA 90035. $15 per year. $22 for institutions.

1.

For sheer energy SULFUR is unique among current
literary periodicals. Each fat issue (approaching some
two hundred pages) features poems, essays, and letters
hitherto unpublished, generally by stars in the
Projective Verse galaxy: <u>Pound, Williams, Olson,
Dahlberg</u>, and <u>Spicer</u>, among them. This work in itself
makes SULFUR essential reading among poets, critics, and
theorists who care about twentieth century American
verse. The current issue, for example, prints a
lengthy exposition on poets by <u>Laura Riding Jackson</u>,
written in a unique and complex prose style. The essay
is a real scoop--this octogenarian former collaborator
and mistress of <u>Robert Graves</u> is a national treasure.
What she says is of primary importance.

There are also unpublished letters by <u>Jack Spicer</u>,
written in the 1950's, to a friend <u>Allen Joyce</u>, and
perceptively edited by <u>Bruce Boone</u>: Spicer casts himself
in lights both fair and foul. Like Riding, Spicer is
another considerable cult writer, one who stands outside
the mainstream of poets approved by academics, the
<u>Halperns, Tillinghasts</u>, and <u>Vendlers</u> of that world.
Almost alone in its influence, SULFUR refocuses light.
SULFUR also has a valuable, iconoclastic, section of
"Notes, Correspondence, Reviews," which I shall comment
on later. Visual art is also featured. #10 highlights
work by <u>Leon Golub</u>, featuring plates for his RIOT II,
1984; five drawings by <u>Anton van Dalen</u>, and prose poems
by <u>Robert Morris</u> accompanying plates of his sculptural
reliefs. The latter works are chosen and commented on
by <u>John Yau</u>, one of the Correspondents.

2.

My focus here is on the poetry, almost all of which is Projective Verse. Each poem is handsomely printed, with much white-space and sizeable type. There is a pretty good mix of known poets (Michael Palmer, Ronald Johnson, Jerome Rothenberg, and Jackson Mac Low have all appeared in SULFUR before.) and of new voices. None of the poems is tightly, ie., conservatively structured or formed--SULFUR's ideal poem has the incandescence of flywheels going off. Many poems are fragments of longer works in progress, viz., Ronald Johnson is represented by the 47th part of his on-going ARK, and Gerald Burns by a substantial chunk of his A BOOK OF SPELLS. Language Poets, represented by Barrett Watten, are fairly balanced.

To see the drift of SULFUR, let's consider Charles Bernstein's brilliant and controversial essay (originally delivered before the staid professor-munchkins of the Modern Language Association Convention, 1983). In "The Academy In Peril: William Carlos Williams Meets the MLA," Bernstein characterizes "the officially sanctioned verse of our time" and laments its "restricted vocabulary, neutral and univocal tone in the guise of voice or persona, grammar-book syntax, received conceits, static and unitary form." He trashes the ultra-conservative and dull poet/critic Richard Tillinghast for encouraging such verse. Poets writing for this "official verse culture, Bernstein points out, "appear regularly in THE NEW YORK TIMES, THE NATION, AMERICAN POETRY REVIEW, NEW YORK REVIEW OF BOOKS, THE NEW YORKER, POETRY (Chicago), ANTAEUS, PARNASSUS, and the Atheneum Press as well as all the major trade publishers. The tie-ins with university writing and lit programs is regrettably clear. Poets usually ignored, or given short shrift by THE HARVARD GUIDE TO CONTEMPORARY AMERICAN WRITING, include Zukovsky, Spicer, Oppen, Reznikoff, Mac Low, Eigner, Riding-Jackson, and Loy. Perceptively and fairly, Bernstein argues that "official verse culture is not mainstream, nor is it monolithic, nor uniformly bad or good. Rather, like all literary culture, it is constituted by particular values that are as heterodox, within the broad context of multicultural American writing, as any other type of writing." It is exactly this alternative tradition that SULFUR reflects, with a tenacity and drive true of no other existing journal.

3.

    Gerald Burns flashes flowers, neon lights, and culture-names with some of the joy of an impish child gone beserk after dark on the Fourth of July. I read along for the pleasures: he sees e. e. cummings' paintings as "inept." On inspecting some lurid flowers ("a pink almost magenta overlain with red-orange") he's reminded of a gilt-bound edition of the Cavalier poet Carew's poems. Other Brit Lit culture-touches flash before our eyes: the arabesques in the Book of Kells; George Moore's CONFESSIONS, that naughty little autobiography of the 1890's; Whistler's Irish model (I assume it's Jo, who was also his mistress, and a model popular with the Moore circle); James (both Henry and William) Ezra Pound; Hogarth; Socrates; and George Borrow of WILD, WILD WALES fame. One admires Burns' well-stocked mind--but we are left wondering what transpires beyond an educated slumming? As good SULFUR poets are apt to do, he speculates on the nature of "language," performing this little jig over Carew's book:

Even unslip-cased
it would have been a widemouth puppet snaffling the
whispered
bits, stroppings of a knife where syllables meet
and another listens, mouth only a little more shut.

This spins from a remarkable imagination, one that loves itself. And it's civilized. When he peels shrimp dipped in a red sauce ("grapes are theology"), the creatures resemble "almond/ skins from the blanching pan, things done to things / pork, hazelnuts in apple, liver dumplings, Tokay." A gormand riff! Here's my favorite line: "One body on a couch, merely digesting, is lonely enough...." Reading Burns' poem, I realize I've had a lot of fun.

    Barrett Watten's "Progress" is from "a book-length work." I hope I am never put in an orgone box and forced to read it. Watten is, of course, one of our more visible spokesmen for the Language Movement, and this slab of a poem (it runs 6 1/2 pages) is pretty typical. He rejects "useless Intelligence," and prefers to run the rabbit-machine backwards, until the rabbits "become hats." I go with this, and thereafter expect much inversion of the "peripheral" world, with its fixed stars, trains arriving on schedule, steams, seas and storms all with logical "connectives." He throws rocks at glass-panes "metrically," and wants "the

figure of invention as/Compensation for private speech."
There's a chilling moment when he realizes that
executioners are sadistic, delaying as they love to do
the "pre-impact terror" before the blade drops.
Analogies create the "stability" Watten desires. The
result, I fear, comes through as sketches, doodlings
almost, produced near Anaheim (was he visiting
Disneyland?):

         A desire to write as inculcated
               By a writer alone in a room
               Only if you can read this
         To produce myself,

                    a dialogue....

         Fixing a voice as it coheres
               On the page,
                         to be adjusted
               I go away and return later
         A distance that equals results....

Watten seems to struggle for originality, and although I
read and reread patiently, I am bothered by the old
chestnuts passing for profundities: "You are only
because you occur / And that is a true thought...." To
be born we must go through "this machine"--mother's
uterus? "Anything named is to be tilted...birds/Point in
the same direction, / Trees stand out in relief...."
Something struggles to get through here, and I wait
cheered by his last line, which says it best: he has
proceeded "With astronomical slowness."

     Bernard Bador's "Sea Urchin Harakiri" is anything
but slow. This excerpt from a work forthcoming from
Panjandrum Press is in the Surrealist mode. As Eshleman
points out in a "Note," Bador's mentors are Tzara and
St. John Perse. His "special morbidity" derives from
Trakl and Benn. His ancestry, traced back to the
notorious Hungarian Blood Countess Elizabeth Bathory
(1560-1614), who bathed in the blood of over 600
virgins, as a means of staying young, figures
subliminally--Eshleman discerns a "coagulate and demonic
power" fluttering through Bador's psyche. His central
image is of a sea urchin "inflicting death upon itself,
using its spines as medieval Japanese samurai ritually
disemboweled themselves." Eshleman finds a parallel with
the Countess who had a special clockwork Iron Maiden
fashioned for decimating virgins. Here's a sampling of
Bador's poems:

         In the shadow of a dot,
         the third eye reddens,

> an acrid almond wandering the snow.

> . . . .

> Suffering stoops the nettles
> deprived of cathedrals,
> but who recalls the rugose acanthi
> of the zodiac, a forger's leprosy
> or a galaxy toll-booth?

Accompanying Bador's work is a set of prose commentaries by Alejandra Pizarnik, on the Blood Countess, translated from the Spanish by Susan Pensak. Also, seven pages from my own forthcoming book of poems, THE BLOOD COUNTESS, written in Bathory's voice, appear.

Jerome Rothenberg continues his labors alerting us to primitive cultures: his "Blood River Shaman Chant" derives from a Finno-Ugric tundra folk, and was chanted by a shaman who worked himself into a trance while slashing his body. The violence and blood are contiguous to Bathory, and with serial murders that have become so much a part of American life.

Jackson Mac Low has been something of a granddaddy of performance artists and language poets. For years, he has written and performed, an iconoclastic, uncompromising poet who avoids the conservative literary spotlights. The two poems here show him as a committed man, on the side of the environment and against nuclear war. "Giant Otters" features Surinam otters, called "Hummers," creatures now loaded with enough trace elements to make them glow: "In even amounts throughout an even eon and an evening more / fortunate as they were in knowing nothing..." The funky style, in the manner of a blandly invented typing-exercise line, is an undercutting of the tragic nature of these now efflorescent beings.

The second poem, "The Psychological Aspects of the Threat of Nuclear War," protests an increasing narcissism which Mac Low sees as "self-interest," the worst of possible actions to take if we are to survive. The "rise of narcissism," he writes, "may reflect underlying death anxiety." The poem, written in long lines (there are playful touches), is revolutionary: we must give up on leaders and "break through the wall of denial above the heads of all governments."

Stephen Rodefer supplies a baker's two-dozen of pretty dull shibboleths, written down monotonously. They seem modelled after maxim books (viz., Voltaire's, or the DEVIL'S DICTIONARY) and rarely dazzle. Here are a few of the better ones: "Masturbation is the absence of

philosophy, it insists on anarchy, but nicely retreats."
"New writing contains propositions not considered
before. Language costumes character, disguising just
another person." "If a cannot equal b, no way can it a
equal either. Any end is always near."

Four short lyrics by George Evans follow. I have
never seen his work elsewhere, and he is a real find.
One poem celebrates the traditional stewed poet (here
the traditional Japanese poet, "the sot Santoka":

        walking, balancing a dragonfly
        on his hat,

        threading and stepping lightly
        over shadows in the pines.

"The Dresser" is about writing also, and boasts a lovely
guise: eschew going the way the world does (ie., the
conventional artists) by placing "gold & near-gold" near
a mirror, "believing it doubled."   Look, Evans says,
at what you really see. "Working for the Iceman" evokes
by-gone days when the iceman made deliveries, and you
assisted, chipping off ice and throwing them to the
kids. Evans does a superb turn on Pleiades, Venus,
authority, and youth. This is the poem:

        He slams the ice down
        small chips fly into yr eyes
        but melt before he beats yr ass
        for crying neon hums
        bugs explode on lights & you pass chunks
        to those chasing the truck before he catches
        on & Pleiades is up there the burlap
        sacks he puts on his shoulder
        flap in the wind the North Star the Bear
        & Venus are out there
        somewhere in the daylight & later
        you'll turn white & die
        but now it's nothing you're young
        and believe he needs you.

Paul Christensen's fourteen-pager, "The Nap," is
original. My interest never flags.   A mother drops off
to sleep. Her son, nearby, meditates on the "green glow
of a cold war, for this is the middle passage of the
1950's, as I report my thoughts to the world during one
of my mother's longer naps":

                I could feel the walls
        turning into flesh, breathing through
        their outlets and old lamps; rooms
        that hollowed like open mouths,
        then curved slowly into pouts.

He relives his rebelliousness. He was a mess,
asthmatic, snaggle-toothed, chinless, hospitalized. He
was his mother's "thin Auschwitz fellow / with his gift
of clogged gab."

The sleeping woman seems afloat on some sea of
life. When she takes her ninth breath (wave), a new
corner of the room glows. The son recalls his first
orgasm:

>   I knead
>   the cold knot in my lap until it stretches
>   numbly on my leg, the forbidden lump
>   knocking upward in its tent of corduroy,
>   the chicken neck that's always left
>   on someone's plate, erect, uneaten
>   bony arc standing up now between
>   tense legs, as if I charmed a snake.
>   No sap--too diluted in my roots;
>   I fear it, feel relief as it gives in,
>   goes flat, cold nub again.

Girl-sex. Life in the grim factory town. Stolen candy.
Punishment. Father at work. The "hot close air of
living rooms." Fear that the mother has died:

>   Mother, wake up. Don't die again,
>   again. Her piston breath still pumping
>   her to life upstairs, in that joyless
>   grave...

The son reverts to grade school, and the atom bomb
school-drills: "Mother, you are a broken branch upon /
the wind; the trees stand withered / in fruitless
seasons of war and peace." He participates in the peace
movement, finally aping his father's career at City
Hall, and swings a plastic briefcase. A sudden painful
wash of awareness--when they are all dead (he now
imagines his mother dead) some tenant will find "one
greasy marble lodged behind/the fridge, last relic of
the family harmony, / the severed knuckle of an /
ancient beast."

His mother "is a fossil in her sleep." Eventually
she wakens, has tea and cookies. She's luridly made-up,
her "ironed dress draped loosely on/her rounded shape,"
ready for receiving her husband, from work. The poem
winds down: we are sojourners in a "fallen world." The
mother's

>   hair hangs limp
>   from all the love she hunted for;
>   the drained emotions form shadows
>   on her lips. I kept vigil

> during her descent, a child-soldier
> guarding his empty gate, while a
> father returns to claim his bed
> my weapons turning into bones and skin.

Marvellous!

Fran O'Farrell writes unpretentiously of herself as "a bottle or woman," and finds herself "thin and infinitely useful." She hopes to make it through the "cotton dawn," diaphanous, "to cloud level." Robert Fitterman also is no show-off: his four lyrics are subtle, taut: one evokes the universal frustration of being stuck in a tourist bus, stalled outside Venice. Another, "The Shelter," is an effective treatment of lovers falling apart, seen through the suburbanite dream (now dissolved) of white-fenced cottage, picture windows, and nice wood floors. The big chunk of Ronald Johnson's epic ARC is not fun to read. The words whizz past without much meaning. Moments of collage whizz past. The ostensible subject is how Ashland, Kansas got its ashes--from an extinct volcano once erupting, primeval (these moments do work). Fashionable references to Rilke, Doughty's ARABIA DESERTA (Doughty is quoted at some length), and a Palazzo tower make us feel well-read and cultured.

Two prose-poems by John Yau are vibrant and bright--he performs some enviable word/image magic over an old photo album with some of the pictures removed-- faded rectangles framed by black ones. The writings once illuminating the disappeared pictures become talismanic moments of "history." Michael Palmer's "Music Rewritten" oscillates around variations on this refrain: "Yes and no then yes and no." Most of the lines sound like starters for inventive popular songs with supporting layers of meaning. The tone is affectionate, even at the end when the lover's (?) face is x-ed out:

> Beneath the shadow of no and yes
> nothing can be said
>
> First there's sameness then difference
> then the letter X across a face
>
> then a line through a name
> which is the wrong name in any case

Palmer's abstractions work. Better than most of the language poets, he provides sufficient narrative hints to locate the reader. This poem (and the prose poem preceding it) remind me of a classic torso of an Apollo, in shards at my feet, each shard gazing up, speaking.

Finally, <u>Ray A. Young Bear</u>'s "Nothing Could Take Away the Bear-King's Image" movingly juxtaposes white culture with native American. Each sees the stars his own way--the white astronomer is enamored of the skies as a chart for Greek gods and goddesses. Young Bear and his friends, two Hispanics, and a Zuni friend sloshed on booze, outside the Griffith Park observatory, in Los Angeles, see the heavens in their own terms. The astronomer has done his best to explain Orion, the Greek hunter to them:

> "I think that's me, Grandfather,"
> responded my Zuni companion,
> "but I will believe you more
> if you sell us your scotch whiskey--
> and consider the magnitude of my belief
> if I told you the bubbles of my Creator's
> saliva made the stars, Grandson."

The astronomer is not amused--the Zuni and the Hispanics bump him "with their expanded chests," and his bagpipes are broken. He weeps. Young Bear and friends flee to the Greek theatre. More ironies--the Zuni National anthem is played under the stars. Police turn up with nightsticks. The poem closes with a panegyric to the permanence of Indian Gods:

> Nothing can take away
> the Bear-king's own image
> who is human and walks.
> There remains a bottle of champagne
> beside the charred concrete block;
> the half-smoked cigarette
> of corn husk and Prince Albert tobacco....

An Indian boy (Young Bear as a child?) is painted black and illuminated with blue spots. Young Bear and friends follow him into an earth-mound, where an Indian Orion (a small man wearing a red headband) sets an arrow "in the bowstring / of his left hand." His message: honor the birds the bison dreams of, the sharp-flint shaft, and the wolfskin draped over the hunter. Young Bear's defiance works because his tale is subtle, mixed in as it is with what the white-world prizes--the world of sky populated by sterile Greek gods. Young Bear is an exciting writer.

4.

A few brief notes on the reviews and other pieces

concluding the volume: following Charles Bernstein's address for the Modern Language Association is Michael Palmer's review of E. Fuller Torrey's THE ROOTS OF TREASON: EZRA POUND AND THE SECRET OF SAINT ELIZABETH'S. Palmer acknowledges a possible double standard for Pound--who was kept from standing trial, abetted by Dr. Winifred Overholser, the superintendent of St. Elizabeths. DADA DATA is an excerpt from J. H. M. C. Boelaars, HEADHUNTERS AMONG THEMSELVES, a list of notes about various parts of the human body, and how the aborigines must regard them: "To touch a man's anus was either an appeal to his strength or a very serious insult." Corpse-ooze was not used for any special purpose, although children were told not to trample the ground where a burial platform had been. A stupid person is a person without ears. Jed Rasula is acute in a lengthy review of the English poet J. H. Prynne, "a formidable talent." Marjorie Perloff rings in with a thorough and devastating reading of Amy Clampitt's poem "Imago": "Clampitt...has loaded every rift with ore to the point that the rifts themselves are safely ignored. We are given so much detail about the sexual evolution of luna moths that we all but lose sight of the central reality of the poet's own sexuality." Perloff is most stimulating on the issue of the closed image poem, totally sanitized and locked in: Clampitt's poetry is "essentially quite mimetic: it makes statements, applies judgments, displays particular prejudices, all the while pretending that these statements cannot be made straightforwardly. Metaphor, as we learned it at school is here decorative rather than integral." There's also a review of Gary Snyder's AXE HANDLES, and a concluding piece by Norman M. Klein on vampires. A fat, rich issue.

<u>TELESCOPE</u>: <u>A</u> <u>JOURNAL</u> <u>OF</u> <u>LITERATURE</u> <u>AND</u> <u>THOUGHT</u>

Vol. III: No. 1 (Winter 1984). Editors: Jack Stephens and Julia Wendell. POB 16129, Baltimore, MD 21218. $9 per year. Distributed by the Johns Hopkins University Press.

TELESCOPE is a young, ambitious journal, fat (c. 175 pp.) with poetry, fiction, essays, and reviews. "Art in the Atomic Age," is the theme. Forthcoming themes are "Cinema and Literature" and "After Einstein."

i.

My concern, once again, is with the poetry. How good is it? Mediocre writing, alas, much outweighs the good. There are thirty-one poems. Over 90% are in that much over-worked mode, the Experience, or First-Person poem, with all the triviality that implies. A couple of these are "You" poems, addressed to persons not present, who for whatever reasons need reminding of what their lives were like. There's a heavy representation of writers with University of Indiana, Iowa, and New Orleans workshop connections. Perhaps this explains so much of the monotony. <u>Henri LePont</u> sits in his "barber's chair / of worry and <u>denial</u>" and writes of "Selaphobia," a fear of light flashes. To adapt one of his lines, his poem "is not epiphany i fear." One of the worst images belongs to <u>Harriet Brown</u>: her thighs "kiss" when she walks, and "<u>sweat collects</u> in arrows" down her sides, "bearing love / from armpit to belly." The lack of what <u>A. C. Swinburne</u> called "tact," a sixth (or seventh) sense by <u>which</u> a poet knows he has written with taste and care and that he conveys the exact tone he desires. How the editors let this poem slip past boggles the mind. Further evidence that Brown can't let well-enough alone, is her report that her sheets "are heavy and continue to mourn / the end of night." If Cannon, Inc. find out, they'll supply Brown with free sheets the rest of her life.

Tactless lines are quite obvious; other defects are subtler. One is the Cultural Veneer, by which some painter or musician is drawn in to assist the poet's solipsistic reportage. <u>Jeanie Thompson</u>'s title itself is a set-up: "<u>allegro assaii</u>." <u>Riding</u> through Arkansas on a dark <u>night with</u> a <u>lover</u>, she drives through a storm. She sets the storm to <u>Bach</u>'s music:

> The storm pulsed _adagio_
> as if in time to the bass,
> the soaring, plaintive violinfire.

I gather that some sort of mystical experience ensued, which Thompson lacks either the language or the imagination to bring off. She settles for this: "I followed as if God had given us / this storm for a beacon." In a similar vein (of Poet as Culture Vulture), _William Olsen_ reports that he is in a boat, his sweetie is sleeping, and he is busy reading _V. Woolf_'s TO THE LIGHTHOUSE. Olsen is a much more seasoned poet than either Brown or Thompson. There's difficulty between the lovers. Olsen ends his lengthy poem movingly:

> Take, love,
> my own name, Bill, meaning
> all the debits and credits
> too gone to know, all the times
> you spoke it, sometimes angrily,
> sometimes like a stringless kite past
> the high wires of conversation,
> up there in the old blue place,
> a gap in the background of all
> we have to turn to beside ourselves.

That's lovely writing--unpretentious, felt.

Keith Ratzlaff contributes one good and two mediocre poems. "Outside Hutchinson, Kansas" details the lives of an aging couple who live over old salt mines. These are potentially lethal, since as they burn, whatever sits above them crumbles. Ratzlaff is too much enamored of the Deep Image. This pair are a bit much: Each rock the man has pulled from the fields leaves "a pocket of air." Cicadas "start sawing the evening in half." In his other poems, Ratzlaff is sentimental and pompous, viz., "A wall needs places in it / that are not wall." When he buys seeds at a feed store, an old man takes his hand and tells him that under the fat there are "good bones." "I believe him," writes Ratzlaff. "From my fingers, / if I were quiet, flowers would rise / that do not want to change the world."

An Obstinate Ordinariness persists in _Michael Garcia-Simms_' work. The bones of "The Answer" run this way: "I have forgotten what I wanted to say...I no longer believe in anything...I turn to you and say i love the world." Anyone for valentines, folks?

Another, far more ambitious poem, _Anneke Campbell_'s "Cranes," also cops out for joy. I wanted this poem to

work; but, alas, in detailing the life of a pregnant
Japanese woman, an "hibakusha," a person exposed to
atomic radiation, Campbell lingers and lingers in the
You Poem mode. She feels obliged to inform the pregnant
woman of her visits to the doctor, of the warnings she'd
received of things to avoid for a healthy pregnancy--X-
rays, children with contagious diseases, coffee, and the
first life she felt in her uterus. The closing lines
show that Campbell can write well. As the bomb
explodes, the Japanese woman observes her mother nursing
a child:

> You watched the nipple come away
> and from the torn breast squirted
>
> red milk. Mother lay down.
> Big black drops of rain began to
> fall on the white mud wall.

The final resolution is similar to one you'd find on a
commonplace TV sitcom. After the MD's examination, the
incipient mother finds that she will have a healthy
baby:

> You want to hug this man in white.
> You want to tell him what might heal
> the crack in the globe.

I don't object to happy endings. Here, though, Campbell
interposes herself obnoxiously between the poem and the
reader, as she pretends to know what the Oriental woman
feels, and what will heal the world. It's just too
facile.

Nothing much happens in Olivia Holmes' poems.
"Dailiness" (the word speaks volumes) contains seventeen
I-phrases and two you-phrases in its fifteen lines. The
effect is thoroughly trivial. She swings the platitude
with the best of them: "Every / night, something sinks,
something rises." She also invents a fey child's world,
one that doesn't synchronize with reality. At the end
of "Vocabulary Exercise," she imagines the inside of a
cloud as a snowflake. It's neither good meterology nor
good poetry:

> The clouds blow like snowflakes,
> but you must believe what I
> say, for they melt before
> we can see their design. We
> only imagine the
> lace heart inside their six sides.

ii

Despite the overwhelming number of maimed poems in TELESCOPE, there are high points. Albert Goldbarth, a master of the solipsistic poem in the contrived and ornate manner, swings easily through the poetry sky on a trapeze of many colors. He's obsessed with foregrounds and backgrounds, as painters are. The real theme, though, seems to be how the protagonist (poet) finds his own shape via the abstract slabs of his life, and has the courage to walk out of a marriage gone awry. Goldbarth is fun to read, even if you don't know what's happening--and he knows that if you mention ice early in a poem it's probably wise to reintroduce it towards the end. But Goldbarth shows off too much; viz., in this image "bedside roses fade to blushes up/ an octopus arm, then back to roses."

One thing very much in TELESCOPE's favor is the absence of family and boyhood/girlhood poems, something of a stock topic with poets emerging from the workshops. Christopher Buckley, a graduate of the MFA program at the University of California, Irvine, writes one of these. The narrative is fairly commonplace--a recollected boyhood experience. I admire Buckley's attempt to translate an early hunting expedition (his friend Harry was superb at shooting doves; Buckley was a klutz) into a statement on violence. They had blasted a jack rabbit to smithereens, simply for the joy of it. Years later Buckley is bothered by this. The message: if you have a gun you'll use it. If you have a nuclear bomb, you'll use it. The NRA will not be happy with this poem.

The discovery here is John Engman who writes superbly within the James Wright/William Staffordian mode of plain-folks remembered. The first poem, "Mushroom Clouds," depicts Miss Nurvak, a teacher, obsessed with the Red Menace, who urges her grade schoolers into safety drills. Engman imagines Nurvak in a bomb shelter:

> In gas mask and green fatigues, Miss Nurvak
> would needlepoint and listen to the gramophone
> until the fatal firestorms passed and she raised
> her periscope, searching for pupils
> from the lost second-grade.

We discover then that the boy who vomited up his Cheerios and who wet his pants in fear was survivor John Engman.

Less successful, but still effective, is

"Asteroids," set in a bar, where the clichés flow and
the TV blares. The barmaids know all of Engman's jokes.
Tiny video-game men holding rayguns steal his spare
change and ravage the earth. Engman makes his stand
"like a vagrant gazing into a flaming / Sterno can."
More barfly buzzings, and this insight:

       The video window is so small only one emotion
 can escape from a face on earth. I try to be brave.

"Transparent Highway Curves" is as moving as any poem
written for a father. Engman's dad "gave his life / to
the slow dissolve of an old Chevrolet sedan." He never
danced, "as he knew he should have"; and he never wanted
to irritate anyone, or fight a war. He sold pencils
"and transparent highway / curves" in Dakota. While he
never wished to be "gay at the Moulin Rouge or sad at
the Ritz," he did wish to protest "conscientiously"
against all that he thought wrong with the world. And
he "wanted his opinions heard by the only audience / he
thought would listen: northern, walleye, bass." Alas,
his sparkpugs got wet, his engine failed, the last bald
tire flattened. When the Chevy stalled, he "didn't just
get philosophical, he walked." He decided that if he
could not change the world, he could change himself:

       Pulling fish from Lake Mille Lacs was his only
       demonstration of force: northern, walleye, bass.
       He sat there in a rowboat, going nowhere, all talk.
       This world, he said, I can't do anything about it.
       He apologized, his voice rising from the water
       into thin air, I can't do anything about it
       echoing, changing planets.

From here on, I'll read all of Engman I can find.

                      iii.

       I am sorry that this review must be bitter-sweet.
TELESCOPE is still a fledgling journal, some three years
old, and the editors are committed to publishing an
ambitious journal with creative and conceptual starch.
If only they were more demanding of their poets. A
defense I often hear from editors who realize that they
publish chaff amongst the gold is that they receive only
so many poems and must fill an issue. Also, the more
writers you print, even if they are mediocre, the more
interest (and subscriptions) you stimulate. Editors
might better serve their cause by expanding the prose
until enough poems of real quality come in to fill the
pages.

<u>THE</u> <u>THREEPENNY</u> <u>REVIEW</u>

Vol. IV: No. 3 (19083).   Editor: Wendy Lesser. Guest
Poetry Editor: Paul Lake.   POB 9131, Berkeley, CA 94709.
Quarterly. $8 per year.

For years now the East Coast has had a stodgy
tabloid aimed at well-educated readers. From its
inception, THE NEW YORK REVIEW OF BOOKS has grayed
itself over. There's always been a smattering of verse,
usually by poets loved by the academy--by <u>Auden</u> and
<u>Lowell</u>, when they were alive, and by <u>Durrell</u> and <u>Graves</u>.

The West Coast equivalent for the NYRB is the THE
THREEPENNY REVIEW, now in its fourth year. Although it
is printed on better-quality paper (it can lie around
your house/study much longer than copies of the NYRB,
before turning brown), it quite self-consciously follows
its model. It does have a lively, if dated, approach to
all the arts. There are reviews of film, dance, music,
art and theater, although literature earns most
attention. In this number, one of 3PR's guiding
luminaries, <u>Robert Pinsky</u>, contributes an essay on
Poetry and Pleasure. <u>Christopher Ricks</u> (doesn't he write
for the NYRB also?) reviews <u>Edward Said</u>'s THE WORLD, THE
TEXT, AND THE CRITIC. <u>Richard Bliss</u> considers a number
of books on <u>James Joyce</u>, who remains a professorial
industry. <u>Dan Bogen</u> supplies a perceptive essay on
Thom Gunn. There's an interview with <u>Derek Walcott</u>,
which, like most interviews, doesn't say much. There
are a couple of short stories (the better one is written
by <u>Dagoberto Gilb</u> "who wears a hardhat in Los Angeles"),
and a review by the editor of CLOUD 9 and PLENTY, months
after their openings in New York. <u>Akhil Gupta</u> writes an
Indian perspective on the film GANDHI over two years
late.   And so it goes. There are nine poems here,
roughly standard for issues of 3PR.

Nearly all the poets are professors: <u>Florence
Verducci</u> teaches at UC Berkeley; <u>Dan Goben</u> is at the
University of Cincinnati; <u>Daniel Mark Epstein</u> is at
Harvard; <u>Paul Lake</u> teaches at Arkansas Tech. Howard
<u>Nemerov</u> is one of the jewels at Washington University,
St. Louis. <u>Miller Williams</u> directs the University of
Arkansas Press and teaches creative writing there. In
contrast, <u>Dana Gioia</u>, "is a businessman in New York."

A quick spin through these poems reveals the pitch.
The editors like verse that assumes cultural knowledge,
if superficial, of readers. Each of the entries below

is adapted from a different poem:

   1. Kronos eats his children. Rhea feeds him a stone. Zeus shears off his genitals.

   2. Moon-seas: Serenitatis, Nectaris, Imbrium, all orchestrated by W. B. Yeats's "unsounded gong."

   3. MADAME BOVARY, L'EDUCATION SENTIMENTAL, Homer, Horace, Baudelaire, Mt. Helicon, Phebe, and Berkeley (California).

   4. Briseis rejected by Achilles obsessed with the dead Patroklos.

   5. Paolo and Francesca.

   6. Dante, Beatrice, and Gemma.

   The remaining poems (three) include one by "business man" Gioia about a businessman's world of walls, desk, swivel chair, calendars, pencils, clock. As you might predict,this is a pretty sterile world:

   Sometimes the shadow of his hand
   Falls from his desk onto the wall
   And is the only thing that moves
   Anywhere at all.

Miller Williams tries out a nice idea--like dolphins we "swim inside ourselves / but we walk on the land." This has a built-in appeal, viz., anyone who has read that book on dolphins thinking like humans, or has seen the documentaries on PBS, is hooked. But Williams can't let well enough alone; he soaks his bed with "sadness" as "a small part of the sea" leaks out his eyes. The resolution is vapid:

   We try to do what's right
   but what do we know?

Australian Les A. Murray scrutinizes a photo of himself, stretching the discoveries over fifteen quietly masterful stanzas. He's gently ironic at his own expense:

   The large ears suggest more
   of the soul than the other features.

His hair "no longer meets across the head." His "chins are firm and deep respectively." His high forehead is so "military-naked" you can "see muscles chewing in the head." This whimsical moment is saved for his eyes:

That look of dawning interest, or objection
in which we glimpse dread of dentists
could be shifting to enjoy a corny joke
out of friendship, or in reflex defiance

of claimant Good Taste and display.

These poems all pay more than passing homage to
traditional forms. All are written in stanzas, all but
one eschew end-rhyme. The most conservative form is
Epstein's--the second and fifth lines of each stanza
have identical rhymes--except for the final couplet-
stanza, which rhymes aa. All poets write in
conventional meters. The basic iamb floats blithely
past, even in poems of varying line lengths. Poems are
damaged by frequently inept Shakespearean turns. There
are no obnoxiously self-indulgent first-person poems.

3PR is, then, has its conservative, audience-elite--
and others need not apply. The SAMISDAT reader will
feel excluded, and vice versa. To apeal to her readers,
the editor seems obliged to review only books and
authors they have possibly already heard of. Thus, if
you are a small press poet the chances of your ever
being reviewed in 3PR are almost non-existent. This
sets up limitations, of course; 3PR is no ground-
breaker. It's brainy and middle-road, and from all
appearances, it will stay that way--a West Coast answer
to the NEW YORK REVIEW OF BOOKS.

YELLOW SILK: JOURNAL OF EROTIC ARTS

#8 (Summer 1983). Editor: Lily Pond. Verygraphics, POB
6374, Albany, CA 94706. Quarterly. $15 per year.

1.

This issue of YELLOW SILK contains over thirty
poems, four stories, an essay, sections of letters and
reviews, and much art work, some reproduced from splashy
19th century graphics of bucolic landscapes and blow-ups
of flowers. Ben Jennings supplies thirteen felt-tip pen
drawings of "flowers and such," in celebration of
penises. Jennings' humor is most welcome in a journal
that takes itself pretty seriously--the poetry, alas, is
not much fun, nor does it rise often above the mediocre.
There's almost a Victorian cast to the verse--you won't
find yourself much titillated by these poets: except for
Miriam Dyak and Arlene Stone. One problem is that
editor Lily Pond likes her erotic verse adorned, nay
overwhelmed, with flowers, trees, and animals:
copulating in forests, cabins, and fields predominates,
a mode of erotic behavior typical of the hippie/flower
children days of the 'sixties. Pond also likes tantric
blends of "the spiritual and the erotic." It's all
pretty tame.

2.

Jan Goodloe, in "Goethe's Theory of Color," opines
that color "is the speech of Nature's soul." In verse
barely a cut above greeting cards, she "speaks" of
larkspur, hyacinth, lavender, cerulean skies, the Black
Hills, and pigeon shimmers. She also summons forth old
Isaac Newton, who obliges her by squinting through a
prism, conjuring "the seven corpuscular substaces," the
"5,000 angstroms/of a scientist's green." The poem
winds down to Goodloe's "milk-white breasts" and her
lover's "amber thighs." Thomas R. Smith announces that
"Nature" has been his "main source" of poetry. His
mushroom poem (guess what, folks, mushrooms are
penises.) crammed with clichés from nature and the
sexual behavior of lupines. Once the lovers return from
a day in the country, they copulate like "children
raised by wolves in the mud and leaves," their nails
"gone back to claws...."

One is grateful for Jeffrey Wilson's poems--they
are short, and he eschews the tedious lists of flora and
fauna we've had so far. But even he, alas, can't resist

finding in nature equivalents for human bodies joined: "The cypress part like lovers' legs / and shiver." A pair of haiku extol labia (I guess) as rose petals "the color of dawn" and a lover's damp "crotch"--a "three o'clock cloud burst" in September. C. W. Spinks, billed as "a mediterranean father of two adopted children, and a compulsive poet addicted to computers," gives no evidence whatsoever that he has read any poetry beyond the late Victorians. If familiarity breeds contempt, this poem, crammed as it is with vapid observations (viz., "the sweet knife of time's sacrifice," "flesh will follow to the grave," "kiss the last sun's pale rays," etc.) resembles a stagnant pond full of mosquito larvae. Dreams, temples, worship, sunrise, and "noon's high tide" don't make it. Rossetti, in his magnificent HOUSE OF LIFE sonnets, understood that such fascinating polarities as body/flesh, body/soul are sterile without fresh and detailed imagery. This Spinks does not know.

Tony Moffeit, "conga-pounding director of the Pueblo Poetry Project," knows a bit more about writing poetry than Spinks seems to. Lovers appear in a landscape drenched with an Apache mysticism and chili (he also spells it chile) peppers adorning his lover's hair. His "ghost vision" of lovers copulating is effective:

> a green corn dance shaking gourd
> shells for the sound of showers
> barbaric drum rhythmic bells fox
> skin and feathers in the hair....

John Minczeski sounds like a poet who's written a lot but not particularly well. An orchid has "a little red vulva" and "a little red penis"; the night is "female"; and there is "so much night" and "so much singing" nobody is able to get to sleep. Buried in these tepid lines is a fresh moment (oh, that there were more!):

> Leaves blacken
> like locust wings that have stopped
> sending messages into the world.

His second poem continues the stock set-up favored by YELLOW SILK: he and his woman make love "in the sun for the first time, / last week." The wind supplies music, and light "falls everywhere." The wind is a "steam engine" pleased with itself. On the way back to the cabin, they drive in their "beat-up Volvo" through the rain. Visions of "shadows" seen earlier in the day wave them through.

At this point (I was at the beach) I was ready to throw YELLOW SILK in the trash can along with empty sun-

tan lotion bottles and used potato chip bags. After a
good dip in the waves, refreshed, I girded up for
another go, turned the page, and found four superb poems
by Miriam Dyak. The nature stuff is all here--edible
plants, zebra and deer, mushrooms, a barn and an old
mattress, roses, milkweed, melons, peaches, apricots,
lemons, persimmons, rock gardens, fossil trails,
salamanders, and bears. For the first time, there's
some real eroticism--a magnificent heterosexual
celebration of an utterly macho male and a vigorous
female who likes her men as men! Dyak loves cock. Her
lover's, just before he comes, tastes like butterscotch.
Better still, his penis is "all 10 mounds of the world's
biggest banana split." Lying beneath him on an old
mattress in a barn, in the missionary position, she
transforms him into an antlered stag:

> I could see the separate hairs   all shades of
>   beige and
>   turning like velvet
> smell thick hide filling space as a mountain
> and blue   sky and clouds roll   through antlers
>   that shoot up like trees beyond
>
> just then you bent your head
>   muzzle softer than rose petals   moth dust
> breath slow ...
> in one gesture I knew all   of power and gentleness
> so my body   broke   as a milkweed in full wind
>   as a stream over the highest rocks
> some feathered seeds   some prismed drops of water
>   still flying
> some part of me entirely gone in air.

Dyak is a terrific lover: excited by her male's skin
texture, taste, and smell (equivalents are numerous
exotic fruits), almost alone, it seems, she induces his
incredible orgasm, "sucking down to the pit / as you
moan out your sweet wild juice." In her fourth poem,
we are treated to his full macho-hood--no quivering poet
esthete he: he "plays Mars on the road" in his four-
wheel drive. He's a hunter, is as "big as a boulder" and
laughs "like a bear." He loves country music. Rough
and tender, that's what he is:

> your touch is sweet and eager as a boy's when he's
>   shot his first deer
> and heaves her still warm across the car   plunges
>   wildly in pure love
> looks down at himself at the blood and sings only her
>   silent cry.

Mary Mackey's direct descendancy from Mark Twain doesn't
seem to improve her poetry much. Here's a particularly

tortured, muddled passage:

     at two thirty-three
     I place the flat of my tongue between your lips
     like a wedge
     my words
     become a school of silver fish
     swimming toward you through the molecular structure
     of your most crystalline dreams
     to feed on the simple darkness
     at the back of the throat...

I'm utterly baffled: how can "the flat" of a tongue make
words that sound like silver fishes? Why the biology
textbook language? Mackey ends up as a dolphin "playing
in the wake" of her lover's breath. More animals,
flowers, and leaves from Marie Henry. Her lovers crawl
on their bellies "looking for tree roots to hide in."

     Arlene Stone, with Dyak, is another of the three
poets worth reading here. "Svengali in Silkwood" is in
Stone's Joycean/Djuna Barnesian style, and is a sizeable
chunk of an epic she has worked on for years. She
makes incredible demands on her reader--and my guess is
that very few readers of SILK have the expertise to stay
with her. Her hero is an idealized Nubian sold as a
slave:

   Color him Midnight   Color he Honey
   Spice   Color hum Wild Rice   frankly for
   myrrincense   Murmur him frangipan   Mirror
   he murmur seas hum from Jamaica Saint
   Thomas   Saint Lucia   triangular trade   rum/
   molasses/slave barques whose hulls be
   hollowed out skulls   white as bone the sea
   chiefs drank of

Stone writes in an argot the Nubian might have himself
used. Here is a passage celebrating his sexuality:

   sex prick dark as the prune womb um
   Africa   Color prick Licorice Color cock
   Emperor purple   him ass um molasses um
   Cleo him sugar cone him rum cunt
   cocktail she wild plums drumdruming him
   sugarcane torso um Color um skin   um
   tattered green rag um colonial flag Sven hum
   reggae hum rosewood cock oaring her
   Sundown   her rum   lakerose/blue/rose/
   blue/rose/blue/rose/blue/rose/blue
       . . . .

   Rhumba the samba mon   sambo he licorice
   stick   voodoo he fuck & lick mon he silk hip

to hip   Sven mon he silkworm him
silkwood   him pearly um touch he um
pineapple penis um knocking she up in Nevis
in Saint Croix Virginny New Orleans....

Stone must be savored. Her rhythms as they echo
primitive dances and primitive speech are uncanny.

A. R. Kazuk contributes six poems. He is vague,
tries to be cerebral, likes sex in nature ("Most like a
birch her body was"; "you curled up/and bound me against
my own tree," "her lips are floral transcriptions/of the
hunger of grade-schools, Braille/for tongues that would
learn by use.") The autobiographical note, written in
incredibly clotted, pretentious prose, warns us that
Kazuk doesn't have much to say: he writes of "a
relationship" he had with a California woman in the
'seventies: "...this passion had its source in the
countries and the times, and not in either of our
personalities. I came to know that sex was the sight
(Kazuk's word) at which an understanding of my place in
the world could be discovered, by a painstaking sifting
of each grain of the sands of the knowledge that I had
been loved and had loved and would do so again." 'Nuff
said!

D. Nurkse commemorates making love in the basement
of a gymn whilst the basketballs thud over-head. Later
on, they take "Time Out" and fuck on a cemetary grave-
slab. A good fuck occurs on Sunday, near a church:
"when the hymn comes on" they "have to grind more
slowly." Joan Seligner Sidney is in her "prime at 40"
and "writes to swallow the world." Alas, her poems
don't show that she's very successful either as
swallower or poet:

I snap the scene indelible. Pass
into the clearing where columbine
pose like women of the night
exposing themselves to all comers

A desert wind poem, in which there's a Loretta Lynn set-
up of a disaffected woman, does end effectively:

I feel you
on my clothes, I
try shaking loose.

Like Dyak and Stone, David Lincoln Fisher seems out
of place here. His "White Nights" is complex. His
trees (an old cypress and a willow) work: there's a
subtle transition from San Francisco to Germany; a
willow over the Neckar river, near Holderlin's Tower,
tells him (as does the cypress) of the nature of love.

He seems estranged from his wife, stands outside her window, merging past and present, Tubingen and San Francisco, and observes a lemon tree brushing its branches against the glass.

Theresa Whitehill reports these goodies: "The ice age of childhood is past." "In your arms you have one of those cracked/marble god women, fine-tuning your liver." I don't think her mother should be proud of these, as Whitehill implies she will be, in her autobiographical blurb. The final poem, an overdrawn effort which reads like a parody of all the easy mysticism, rosy-crucianism, seer-icizing of the flower children days, is by Cheri Lesh, a.k.a. Cerridwen Fallingstar, "an Erisian Priestess living in Mill Valley," a member of Holy Terror Coven, mother to Zachary Moonstone. The first night she made love to her "blood sister," the woman bled "all night." During their sleep, they had "uterine converations."

Perhaps, to be fair, I might see writing in YELLOW SILK as consciously amateurish--the editor has an unsophisticated readership in mind. These are the same readers who buy up the wretched books of verses perpetrated by Suzanne Somers, Leonard Nimoy, Ray Bradbury, Hugh Prather, Richard Thomas, Susan Schutz and their ilk. And it is possible that this is the audience Lily Pond, the editor aims to reach. There is, I feel, the smell of the Collective about YELLOW SILK--as long as the work is by a subscriber or someone on the mast-head, and it isn't utterly wretched, publish it. That Pond has pretensions to literary quality does, though, seem obvious: not only does she showcase a lot of poets per issue, but past issues have included work by some fairly prestigious folk, viz., Susan Griffin, Ntozake Shange, Lyn Lifshin, Genet, Frank O'Hara, Wanda Coleman, Jessica Hagedorn, W. S. Merwin, Frank Polite, and Paul Mariah. My hope is that the editor will educate herself as to quality in poetry. Another solution is to appoint a poetry editor of some taste and achievement. As the journal reaches an ever wider audience, perhaps more good poets will contribute work. I hope so. I also wish the eroticism were more imaginative and controversial--forget fucking in the woods and fields-- or at least, cut those nature settings down to a few poems per issue. Lily Pond might take a look at a journal like the FAG RAG, out of Boston, which flirts always with the outrageous, and publishes a healthy mix of turn-on poems plus poems of literary merit. YELLOW SILK could serve far more of a purpose than it does--by striving to expand our erotic consciousness--by daring to be more controversial and less clichèd than it is.

THE BLACK AND BLUE GUIDE NOISOME BUNNY AWARDS

BEST: Bluefish, Contact II, Sulfur

GOOD: Bogg, Connecticut Poetry Review, Electrum, New
Letters, Pulpsmith, Permafrost, Samisdat

MIDDLING: Bellingham Review, Grand Street, Gypsy,
Magazine, Massachusetts Review, Paris Review, Poetry
Review, Telescope, Threepenny Review

NOISOME: Graham House Review, Ironwood, Yellow Silk

m. peters

INDEX

ROBERT PETERS, **Hawker**

photograph by Michael Elderman

ROBERT PETERS, a prolific and well-regarded author for the past fifteen years, recently created a new form of book-length poems, each centered around an historical character. The gallery of these "voice portraits," as he has named them, includes Mother Ann Lee (founder of the Shakers), Ludwig of Bavaria, Lord Byron and, now, Robert Stephen Hawker, Vicar of Morwenstowe, Cornwall, in the nineteenth century. The next portrait, KANE, will be published by Unicorn Press in 1985.

Peters was born on a farm in Wisconsin and now lives near a beach in Southern California. Recently he adapted *Picnic in the Snow: Ludwig of Bavaria* and *Hawker* into stage versions in which he himself acts. When he is not on tour with these works, he teaches Victorian literature at the University of California in Irvine.

HAWKER was awarded the Poetry Society of America's Alice Faye di Castagnola Prize in 1982.

Unicorn Foundation, Inc.
P.O. Box 3307
Greensboro, North Carolina 27402

ROBERT STEPHEN HAWKER (1802-1875) was Vicar of Morwenstowe in Cornwall. He lived all his life in this wild and desolate parish near the high, jagged cliffs of the Cornish coast, noted for its shipwrecks. Hawker, poet, essayist, individualist, was obsessed with rescuing drowned sailors; he dressed eccentrically by day, played at being a mermaid by night, took opium in later life...and left a body of writing and legend behind him, from which Peters has drawn for one of his unique "voice portraits."

Hawker of Morwenstowe

$ 7.00 paper 0-87775-166-8

$15.00 cloth 0-87775-165-X

115 pages, illustrated cover

smyth-sewn; handbound

CRITICS ON PETERS' *GREAT AMERICAN POETRY BAKE-OFF*: Series I and II. Scarecrow Press, Metuchen, NJ.

"I like Peters because his criticism is not maternal; many poets he writes of attack him on precisely that point. But I think it's up to our friends to encourage us, and for strangers, by assuming a few lumps will not hurt us, to confront us . . . The essay on Creeley is superb; the best essay on his work I know." —Robert Bly, *The American Book Review.*

"Peters knows how to keep the readers awake; there's not a single yawn in his book." —Marjorie Wentworth, *Touchstone.*

Peters . . . earns his reader's consent to the truth of his witty rhetoric with provocatively chosen illustration . . . one of the best volumes of modern poetry criticism to appear in the seventies." —*Choice.*

" . . . the finest contemporary guide to the art of poetic criticism this reviewer has recently seen." —Kenneth Funsten, *Library Journal.*

"Peters gives to . . . poetry precisely the independent, serious but also barbed attention it cries for." —*Small Press Review,* Book Club Selection.

"Robert Peters is a much published poet who is also an exciting critic and teacher. This new book of his literary essays . . . ought to increase that reputation. The views here are trenchant and well developed." —Susan Shafarzek, *Library Journal.*

"When Peters points out the cliches in poems by established poets . . . you may smile at first, but later you'll check over your own work. A good critic is hard to find." —Richard Peabody, *Gargoyle.*

"Peters, long among our most fearless yet responsible critics, metes out high praise where high praise is earned. He has no respect, however, for overinflated reputations . . ." —*Samisdat.*

"In this remarkable book . . . Peters is not above slang and harangue, though he always shows great care and a desire to be constructive, even in the harshest railleries—he'll have you rolling in the idols/idylls." —Tom Peterson, *San Francisco Review of Books.*